DEVELOPING POSITIVE STUDENT SELF-CONCEPT

Second Edition

David L. Silvernail

nea PROFESSIONAL LIBRARY
National Education Association
Washington, D.C.

Note

The opinions expressed in this publication should not be construed as representing the policy or position of the National Education Association. Materials published as part of the Analysis and Action Series are intended to be discussion documents for teachers who are concerned with specialized interests of the profession.

Printing History:
First Edition
First Printing: January 1981
Second Printing: September 1984
Second Edition
First Printing: January 1985

Library of Congress Cataloging in Publication Data

Silvernail, David L.
Developing positive student self-concept

(Analysis and action series)
Bibliography: p.
1.Student—Psychology. 2. Self-perception.
I. Title. II. Series.
LB1117.S474 1985 371.8'1 85-327
ISBN 0-8106-1692-0

Contents

SELECTED RESOURCES FOR THE SECOND EDITION

Alban Metcalfe, R. J., and Alban Metcalfe, B. M. "Self-Concept, Motivation, and Attitudes to School Among Middle School Pupils (Great Britain)." *Research in Education* 26 (November 1981): 64–76.

Alston, D. N., and Williams, N. "Relationship Between Father Absence and Self-Concept of Black Adolescent Boys." *Journal of Negro Education* 51(Spring 1982): 134–38.

Battle, J., and Blowers, T. "Longitudinal Comparative Study of the Self-Esteem of Students in Regular and Special Education Classes." *Journal of Learning Disabilities* 15 (February 1982) 100–102.

Beane, J. A. "Self-Concept and Self-Esteem as Curriculum Issues." *Educational Leadership* 39 (April 1982): 504–6.

______. "Self-Concept and Esteem in the Middle Level School." *NASSP Bulletin* 67 (May 1983): 63–71.

______, et al. "Synthesis of Research on Self-Concept." *Educational Leadership* 38 (October 1980): 84–89.

Beier, B. "Enhancing Positive Self-Concept Through Creativity in the Classroom." *Health Education* 12 (March/April 1981): 35.

Bernstein, R. M. "Relationship Between Dimensions of Delinquency and the Development of Self and Peer Perception." *Adolescence* 16 (Fall 1981): 543–56.

Burnett, P. C. "A Self-Concept Enhancement Program for Children in the Regular Classroom." *Elementary School Guidance and Counseling* 18 (December 1983): 101–8.

Byrne, B. M. "Investigating Measures of Self-Concept." *Measurement and Evaluation in Guidance* 16 (October 1983): 115–26.

Coleman, M., and Fults, B. A. "Self-Concept and the Gifted Classroom: The Role of Social Comparisons." *Gifted Child Quarterly* 26 (Summer 1982): 116–20.

Crosby, R. "Self-Concept Development." *Journal of School Health* 52 (September 1982): 432–36.

Dobson, J. E., et al. "Relationship Between Children's Self-Concepts, Perceptions of School, and Life Change." *Elementary School Guidance and Counseling* 17 (December 1982): 100–107.

Dusek, J. B., and Flaherty, J. F. "Development of the Self-Concept During the Adolescent Years." *Society for Research in Child Development.* Monograph 46, no. 4 (1981): 1–67.

Eder, D. "Ability Grouping and Students' Academic Self-Concepts: A Case Study." *Elementary School Journal* 84 (November 1983): 149–61.

Fleming, P. "The 'Quiet' Wave: Changes in Self-Concept on Entering School." *School Guidance Worker* 39 (January 1984): 15–19.

Frantz, M. K. "Strengthening the Self-Concept Through Creative Movement Activities." *Physical Education* 40 (March 1983): 42–43.

Glazzard, P. "Building Self-Concepts." *Early Years* 12 (September 1981): 74+.

Gottsdanker-Willekens, A. E., and Leonard, P. Y. "All About Me: Language Arts Strategies to Enhance Self-Concept." *Reading Teacher* 37 (April 1984): 801–2.

Graham, T. L., and Knight, M. E. "How to Promote a Postive Self-Concept." *Early Years* 14 (August/September 1983): 40–41+.

Herzberger, S. D., et al. "Developmental Study of Social Self-Conceptions in Adolescence: Impressions and Misimpressions." *Merrill-Palmer Quarterly* 27 (January 1981): 149–57.

(Continued on page 65)

AUTHOR'S PREFACE TO THE SECOND EDITION

In preparing for the publication of this second edition, I reviewed the Introduction to the first edition thinking that some of my original comments might no longer be applicable. I have concluded, however, that those comments are as relevant today as they were at the time of the first publication.

The country has moved into a conservative era. With it has come a reexamination of the purposes and roles of education and schooling in American society. Several recent reports, for example, have lamented the state of education and offered a plethora of recommendations for improving the educational system. The initial response in many instances has been a flurry of legislative mandates for improving the academic performance of students.

Although well intentioned, many of these mandates, if viewed narrowly, limit the role of educators. As the first edition noted, from time immemorial educators have been given the responsibility for educating the whole child—caring for the personal and social as well as the intellectual development of students. It is essential not to lose sight of these goals as attempts are made to respond to the often narrow prescriptions being offered. Quite the contrary, educators must renew their efforts to identify ways to enhance not only the intellectual development, but also the personal and social well-being of students. One way to achieve these goals is to help students develop positive self-concepts.

This publication reviews the empirical research to assist educators in increasing their understanding of self-concept development and to identify effective strategies for developing positive student self-concepts. The second edition includes a number of recent sources that complement the material presented in the first edition. In addition, I would like to call attention to three of the Selected Resources for the Second Edition: *Self-Concept: Advances in Theory and Research* (edited by Lynch et al.), *Social Psychology of the Self-Concept* (edited by Rosenberg and Kaplan), and *Self-Concept in the Young Child: An Anthology* (edited by Yawkey). These books will be particularly helpful in providing a more thorough and fundamental understanding of self-concept development. They can serve as valuable supplements to the research described here.

I hope the material presented in the following pages, together with the references, will assist educators in identifying effective ways to educate the whole child. This is not an easy task, but it is one of paramount importance to the future of our society.

D. L. S.

The Author

David L. Silvernail is Director of the Student Testing and Assessment Center at the University of Southern Maine, Portland. He is also the author of *Teaching Styles as Related to Student Achievement,* published by NEA.

The Advisory Panel

James Blank, sixth grade teacher, Cleveland Elementary School, Manitowoc, Wisconsin

Rita Hodgkins, Media Specialist, Louis Pasteur Intermediate School, Sacramento, California

Donald R. Nelson, Head, Teacher Education, Louisiana Tech University, Ruston

Alan D. Rozinsky, Psychology Instructor, Social Studies Department, Weaver High School, Hartford, Connecticut.

INTRODUCTION

"Educate the whole child." This maxim has been and continues to be the guiding light of American education. Historically, educators have had four kinds of goals: (1) academic; (2) vocational; (3) social and civic; and (4) personal, including self-concept development (77). Evidence of the four can be found in such earlier works as *Cardinal Principles of Secondary Education* published in 1918 and *The Purposes of Education in American Democracy* published in 1938 (39, 57). More recently, identical goals have surfaced in attempts to synthesize the views of various educational constituencies (77, 124). Thus, at least on paper, it can be said that these four goals are the primary reason for our educational endeavors.

Throughout history, however, social and economic conditions have influenced the amount of emphasis given to certain goals. During particular periods, some goals have received precedence over others. In the early part of this century, for instance, academic goals were a primary concern. In the 1930s concern shifted to social and personal goals until the 1960s after Sputnik, when it returned to an academic focus. Following this period, the rise of the "humanistic" movement saw a reemphasis on the personal and social (152).

For two decades humanistic education has been riding the crest, but some fear it is threatened by the current interest in back-to-basics and competency testing. Others do not agree (118). They theorize that the public still wants educational institutions to be concerned with the personal and social development of their children. And empirical evidence supports their claim. A recent survey of teachers and administrators revealed that the development of a positive self-concept on the part of students is still a very important goal in the eyes of these educators (157). A similar survey of teachers and *parents* asked these groups to rate the importance of four broad goals and to indicate which ones should be emphasized most in our schools. All four were viewed as important with personal goals ranking second only to intellectual ones in terms of needed emphasis (77, 98).

Thus, it is apparent that our concern for helping youth develop intellectually must not overshadow an equally important concern for their personal development. As educators, then, it behooves us to identify strategies for developing and enhancing the self-concepts of our students. Fortunately, during the past two decades more and more researchers have turned their attention to this subject. The result has been an almost exponential growth in research on student self-concept. Unfortunately, however, most of the research findings have not reached the hands of the classroom teacher. Many reasons can be cited for this breakdown in communication, but paramount among them is the fact that the findings often appear in journals and references not readily accessible to the classroom teacher. The purpose of this publication is to take at least one step toward correcting this situation. More specifically, the intent is to provide a brief and, it is hoped, concise review of the state of the art and science of self-concept development. The final section includes practical suggestions gleaned from the research and literature that may aid the teacher in the process of developing and enhancing the self-concepts of students.

DEFINITIONS

Before turning to a review of the literature, it is important to define the term 'self-concept'. This is not an easy task, for even a cursory review of existing theories and research studies reveals a multitude of different definitions, some more precise and exacting than others. 'Self', for instance, has been defined as "that which is designated in common speech by the pronouns of the first person singular, 'I', 'me', 'mine' and 'myself' " (41). Others have defined 'self-concept' in a similar manner: "the organization of all that seems to the individual to be 'I' or 'me' " (38). 'Self' has also been defined as "a complex and dynamic system of beliefs which an individual holds true about himself, and each belief with a corresponding value" (134). Still other definitions of 'self-concept' include "a person's perceptions of himself" (152) and "what an individual believes about himself, the totality of his ways of seeing himself" (35).

Turning for a moment to 'self-esteem', a word often used interchangeably with self-concept, it has been described as "a positive or negative attitude toward a particular object, namely, self" (138) and as "feelings of personal worth . . . influenced by performance, abilities, appearance, and judgments of significant others" (59). And to demonstrate the interchangeability of the two terms, 'self-concept' has been defined as "the sum total of all of the characteristics a person attributes to himself, and the positive and negative values he attaches to these characteristics" (136).

Many more definitions could be cited, each slightly different, but this quickly becomes a futile exercise. Accordingly, at least on the surface, there appears to be some confusion regarding the definition of terms (27, 73). Upon closer examination, however, some distinctions do emerge. First, 'self' is distinguishable from 'self-concept'. The most widely accepted definition of 'self' is the one first cited (41). It is referred to as the "looking-glass self" — the idea that we perceive ourselves as reflected in a mirror. As we become aware of our reflection, we become aware of our 'self' (that is, we begin to use expressions such as 'I', 'me', and 'mine'). As we become aware of 'self', we begin to perceive ourselves in terms of roles, abilities, limitations, etc. These perceptions are, in part, self-determined, and, in part, influenced by the way we believe others perceive us. Some theoreticians (69, 114, 165) believe these perceptions are strongly influenced by the "significant others" in our lives, while others (72, 107) believe the major influence is derived from identifications we make with particular social groups. In all probability it is not an either/or situation — both are likely to influence our views.

Thus, 'self-concept' can be defined as the way we perceive ourselves and our actions, and our opinions regarding how others perceive us. As such, our self-concept is multifaceted. For instance, we perceive ourselves in different roles (child, student, parent) with different abilities (physical, mental) and different limitations. All these are subparts of our self and combine to form our general self-concept. Generally, theoreticians and researchers believe the key dimensions of the general self-concept are the sense of (1) body self, (2) cognitive self, (3) social self, and (4) self-esteem. The first three dimensions are self-explanatory, but the fourth dimension needs clarification.

Self-esteem is the evaluative dimension of our self-concept. While our self-concept describes our perceptions, or self-esteem evaluates these perceptions. In essence, it is the value we place upon the various dimensions of our general self-concept. This suggests that our self-concept develops earlier than our self-esteem — we perceive our 'self' in certain ways (roles, abilities, etc.) and then we develop an evaluation of these self-images. Accordingly, we may have an accurate self-concept and either a positive or negative self-esteem concurrently.

Pulling this discussion together, then, we first perceive our 'self' as a separate entity. As we do, we begin to describe our self in terms of roles, abilities, and specific attributes; that is, we develop a 'self-concept'. This self-concept is composed of many images, or dimensions. One dimension is 'self-esteem', the values we assign to each role, ability, attribute.

Given these definitions and distinctions, we can now describe some additional features of 'self-concept' (152).

1. The self-concept is *multidimensional*. It includes many subparts, and even these subparts may have more than one dimension. For example, one subpart may be labeled our physical self-concept. But the physical self-concept can be further divided into our perceptions of our physical appearance, physical ability, etc.

2. The self-concept is *hierarchical*. Certain descriptions and evaluations form the core of our self-concept; that is, they are closer to the essence of our self. For instance, our image as "teacher" may be more central to our being than our image as "golfer."

3. The self-concept, at least the general self-concept, is fairly *stable*. Our core perceptions develop early and change little through time. A long history of inconsistent perceptions is needed before these 'selfs' change. However, as we descend the self-concept hierarchy — that is, move away from the core images — the self-concept becomes less stable. Our physical self-concept is set early and maintains a certain stability, but our perceptions of our physical appearance or agility, for example, change fairly easily with time, growth, and events.

4. Finally, the self-concept is *evaluative*. Not only do we develop a description of our self, but we also formulate evaluations of this description. These evaluations placed in the context of the other three features just described, suggest that the core evaluations are developed early in life and are resistant to change. Other less significant evaluations are constantly being developed, modified, discarded, and replaced by others.

To summarize, and for the purposes of this publication, a *self-concept is defined as a person's perception of himself/herself*. This perception is multidimensional, hierarchical, fairly stable, and evaluative. Clearly, this description cannot be viewed as an all-inclusive definition of self-concept. Even if we accept these four as the salient features, unquestionably the total is greater than the sum of the parts. But recognition of even these features may help to make us mindful, as teachers, of the tremendous task before us. How can we develop strategies that will effectively enhance a child's self-concept? Moreover, how do we effectively enhance the self-concepts of many children, each one coming to us with a different self-concept, and each one having a self-concept that is fairly well defined by the time he/she reaches our classroom? Before turning our attention to the strategies, therefore, it becomes apparent that we need to understand the early development of a child's self and self-concept. Accordingly, the next section describes, in capsule form, what we know about the early years.

First, however, one caveat is in order — applying not only to the next section but to subsequent ones. This section has attempted to make some distinctions regarding self-prefixed terms. It is hoped that these distinctions will be helpful to the reader, but it must be recognized that there is not total agreement on terminology. The definitions given bear this out and, unfortunately, many times educators and researchers use self-prefixed terms interchangeably. For instance, researchers will attempt to measure self-concept using scales designated as self-esteem measurements. The review and analysis of the literature which follow are based, as much as possible, on the definition of self-concept given here.

EARLY SELF-CONCEPT DEVELOPMENT

In essence, self development begins at birth. The child is not aware of being a separate being, a self, but within seconds after birth, the child begins to interact with his/her environment. Gradually, the infant begins to develop simple patterns of perception and action followed by more complex ones, and within a few weeks begins to become aware of his/her existence as a separate entity. One study reports that the first signs of separation from the mother begin in the third or fourth month after birth (109. Quickly the child begins to see himself/herself as separate from other people and within a few months begins to assign a perception to his/her self (159).

Once the self is perceived and language acquisition begins, the core dimensions of the self-concept begin to formulate quickly. Obviously, the first few years are crucial in a child's development, physically, socially, and intellectually. Equally important is the value the youngster places on his/her perceptions and the perceptions of others.

In very large measure, the environment the child interacts with early in life establishes the core self-concept, the perceptions which make up the general self-concept. Unquestionably, the parental care received in the early years plays an enormous role in defining the child's self-image. A supportive environment, with many stimuli and visible love and care on the part of parents, will enhance the development of a psychologically sound and stable self-concept. An opposite environment will, in all likelihood, contribute to the development of children who are psychologically crippled

The significance assigned to parental care should not be underestimated. One study found that the child's level of self-regard is related to his/her parents' level of regard for the child (110). Another reported that kindergarten pupils who exhibited high self-esteem came from homes in which mothers encouraged autonomy and independence on the part of the children (50). Furthermore, the impact of early parental care extends beyond the formative years. A seven-year followup study of five-year-olds reported that those who came from homes where high parental warmth existed had higher self-concept levels at age twelve (148). And another researcher found that children not only rank their parents as "significant others" during early childhood, but continue to rank them as important "significant others" throughout the adolescent years (19).

Thus early parental care has a tremendous impact on the self-concept development of children. Specifically, what type of care? A fairly definitive answer can be found in the seminal study by Coopersmith (42). As a result of his extensive seven-year examination of the experiences and conditions associated with the development of self-esteem, this researcher was able to isolate three conditions that distinguished high from low self-esteem development. These three conditions, along with Coopersmith's generalized findings, are as follows:

1. *Total or nearly total acceptance of the children by their parents:* They (the findings) reveal that the mothers of children with high self-

esteem are more loving and have closer relationships with their children than do the mothers of children with less self-esteem. . . . The greater acceptance of the child with high and medium self-esteem is manifested by interest, concern about companions, availability, and congenial joint activities. The child apparently perceives and appreciates the attention and approval expressed by his mother and tends to view her as favoring and supportive. He also appears to interpret her interest and concern as an indication of his significance; basking in these signs of his personal importance, he comes to regard himself favorably. (42:178–79)

2. *Clearly defined and enforced limits:* The conditions that exist within the families of children with high self-esteem are notable for the demands the parents make and the firmness and care with which they enforce those demands. Reward is the preferred mode of affecting behavior, but where punishment is required, it is geared to managing undesired responses rather than to harsh treatment or loss of love. . . . The total amount of punishment administered in these families is not less than in others, but it is different in its expression and is perceived as justifiable by our high self-esteem subjects. (42:196)

3. *Respect and latitude for individual action:* The results point to a negative relationship between the limits established for the child and the freedom he is granted within those limits. Thus, we find that the families of children with high self-esteem not only establish the closest and most extensive set of rules, but are also the most zealous in enforcing them. This establishes the authority of the parent, defines the environment, and provides standards by which the child can judge his competence and progress. Parental treatment within these limits is noncoercive and recognizes the rights and opinions of the child. His views are sought, his opinions are respected, and concessions are granted to him if differences exist. The latitude that prevails within the general limits permits the child to enter into discussions as a significant participant and to gain the benefits of self-assertion. (42:213–14)*

---

*Stanley Coopersmith, *The Antecedents of Self-Esteem* (San Francisco: W. H. Freeman and Co.), © 1967. Reprinted by permission of Alice Coopersmith, Administratrix of the Estate of Stanley Coopersmith.

Other researchers have uncovered evidence which supports Coopersmith's findings, such as a significant relationship between parental positive attention and adolescents' self-esteem (138), and a positive relationship between parental acceptance of children and children's self-evaluations (84). Still others have found that high-anxiety-level children had fathers who tended to be harsh in their parental judgments (94); and particular types of parental evaluations led to higher anxiety levels and more negative self-concepts on the part of children (146). Specifically, mothers who evaluated the child in terms of the mother's needs, rather than the child's needs, had children who exhibited more anxiety and lower self-concepts.

Investigators have also discovered that parental self-concept, particularly maternal self-concept, is related to child rearing practices and child self-concept development. Mothers who possessed positive self-esteem tended to show greater affection and warmth toward their children (150); and mothers who were more self-accepting showed more approval and acceptance of their children (115). Other studies revealed that highly anxious children came from homes in which the mothers were more anxious (1), and mothers' self-concepts were positively related to their children's self-concepts (169).

Thus, the impact of early parental care on self-concept development can be summarized in a nutshell: it is tremendous and long lasting. Parents who possess positive self-images create an environment which promotes positive self-concept development on the part of their children. In a supportive environment, one which promotes affection, warmth, and respect between parent and child, and one with clearly defined rules and expectations of behavior, children will have a very good chance of developing a psychologically healthy self-image. The opposite environment will, in all likelihood, create self-images which are psychologically damaged. Consequently, the care a child receives in the early years prior to attending school in very large measure sets the stage for the future development of his/her self-concept. It establishes the core self-image and thereby influences what will happen to the child's self-concept as he/she becomes a student in our schools.

SCHOOLING AND SELF-CONCEPT DEVELOPMENT

What happens to a child's self-concept once s/he begins attending school? Essentially, this can be considered a two-part question. First, what happens in the normal course of events, or, to put it another way, what school variables are related to student self-concept? Second, what are the results when strategies and activities designed specifically to enhance student self-concept are introduced into the curriculum? This section attempts to answer the first question, and the subsequent section addresses the second.

The Impact of School Variables on Student Self-Concept

The relationship of school variables to student self-concept has received a great deal of attention by researchers in recent years. A review of the literature reveals that investigators have attempted to explore this question from almost every angle. Many attempts have proved fruitless; but, by the same token, many have proved fruitful. Therefore, we are beginning to get a clearer picture of what variables are associated with student self-concept. Before describing them, however, a cautionary note is in order. It should be pointed out that most of the research reported in this section deals with correlational findings. A correlational study establishes the presence or absence of a mutual relationship, but it cannot determine cause and effect. Thus, for example, when a study reports that teacher businesslike behavior is correlated or related to higher self-concept, it tells us that when businesslike behavior is present, in all likelihood higher student self-concept is also present. It does not tell us that businesslike behavior *causes* higher student self-concept. The casual relationship may or may not exist, but this can be determined only through the use of an experimental design. Most of the studies reported in this section are correlational in nature, while many experimental studies are described in the subsequent section. With this in mind, let us now turn our attention to the research that has attempted to explore the relationships between schooling variables and self-concept.

As educators, we would like to believe that everything we do relates in a positive way to self-concept development. Unfortunately, this belief is not supported by the empirical evidence. It appears that our actions affect students differently. For example, we know that for some students their self-concept becomes more positive during the schooling years and for others it becomes more negative. One study reports that for many students the trend is toward acquiring more negative self-images with each additional year of schooling (7). Using various forms of the *Index of Adjustment and Values*, designed to measure perceptions of self and others, the researcher surveyed the perceptions of approximately twenty-six thousand students in grades three through twelve and concluded:

> The data show developmental trends. Although some of these changes appear to be of a positive nature, the data overwhelmingly support the conclusion that progressive deterioration is present in perceptions of self and other people and in adherence to a set of values, many of which are of basic importance in human welfare and relationships. In short, the data picture of the developmental trends in self-concept variables [is] negative leading to doubts about self-worth and the worth of other people, to increased defensiveness, and to rejection of values which are basic to feelings of worth, beliefs in the dignity and worth of other people, adequate interpersonal relationships and principles of behavior. (7)

These findings are supported by the research of other investigators who administered the *Self Observation Scale*, an instrument designed to measure self-concept in primary and intermediate school children, to approximately thirty-seven hundred primary students in grades one through three (161). To the query "Are you good-looking?" 25 percent of the first graders and almost 50 percent of the third graders answered in the negative. Twenty percent of the first graders thought other children in their class disliked them and 28 percent believed other people did not like their ideas. According to the third graders, 30 percent thought they were disliked by other classmates, and 36 percent believed their ideas were not liked by others. Eighty percent of the first graders and only 67 percent of the third graders thought they were doing as well as they should in their work. The investigators also report that while approximately 90 percent of the total sample reported their teachers liked them, fewer third graders than first graders felt this way.

Additional evidence indicates that this decline in self-concept continues into the upper grades. A survey of over six hundred students in alternate grades from three through eleven found a decline in self-esteem (121). When presented the item "I'm pretty sure of myself," 88 percent of the third graders said "like me," but only 66 percent of the eleventh graders responded in a similar manner. Eighty-four percent of the third graders were proud of their work and over half felt they were doing as well in school as they would like. For the eleventh graders, 53 percent were proud of their school work and only 22 percent thought they were doing as well in school as they would like. Finally, in the early grades, 93 percent of the students believed they were doing the best work they could, while only 37 percent of the oldest students felt the same way.

The empirical findings therefore lead to the conclusion that schooling affects children's self-concepts differently. For some children, the effects are in a positive direction; for others the effects are negative. What determines the direction the effects will take? At least a partial answer may be found in the relationships known to exist between certain school characteristics and student self-concept. Let us turn our attention, first, to academic characteristics.

Numerous researchers have examined the relationship between academic achievement and self-concept. With a few exceptions, the findings have indicated a significant and positive relationship between the two variables. High self-concept is concomitant with high achievement, low self-concept with low achievement. For instance, high-achieving intermediate grade students were found to have significantly higher general self-concepts and academic self-concepts than low-achieving cohorts (60). Similar findings were reported for the relationship between reading and mathematics achievement and self-concept (176). And a study of eleventh grade over- and underachievers revealed that students who exhibited high academic productivity levels tended to have higher self-concepts (61). Other researchers found underachievers with more negative self-concepts than achievers (64, 153), and seeing themselves as less adequate (37, 53).

At first glance these differences in self-concept levels of achievers and underachievers might appear to be attributable to differences in intelligence. However, a study involving over one thousand seventh graders found that the positive relationship between achievement and self-concept remains intact even after IQ scores are factored out of the data analysis (19). Also, evidence uncovered by other researchers reveals that intelligent underachieving high school male students have more negative self-concepts than students of equal intelligence who are achieving at their ability levels (154). Thus, it is safe to conclude that achievement and self-concept are related and the relationship cannot be accounted for solely on the basis of intelligence.

Teacher characteristics have also been found to be related to student self-concept. Two studies discovered that students' perceptions of their teachers' feelings toward them are highly correlated with self-perceptions (44, 101). Students who feel they are liked and respected by their teachers have higher self-concepts, while those who believe they are disliked by their teachers are more dissatisfied with themselves. Morevoer, some evidence suggests that these student perceptions may be a reflection of teachers' self-perceptions. For instance, researchers report that lowering of student self-esteem is positively related to teacher self-esteem (55).

Two additional studies give us a clearer picture of the relationship between teacher characteristics and student self-concept. In the first study Spaulding conducted an extensive survey of teacher-student transactions in elementary schools, using classroom observations to categorize teacher-student transactional patterns in 21 fourth and sixth grade classes (160). These patterns were correlated with measures of achievement, creativity, and self-concept. With respect to self-concept correlations, significant relationships were found for "socially integrative" and "learner and supportive" teacher behaviors, specific characteristics of "democratic" leader behavior, and other teacher behaviors. More specifically, a positive relationship was found between student self-concept and one component of "socially integrative" behavior described by earlier researchers (4). This component is "calm, acceptant transactions, in general, with private, individualized instruction and a concern for divergency, attention to task, and the use of task appropriate procedures and resources." A similar relationship was found for the "learner-supportive" category of teacher behavior (177), a category defined much like the "socially integrative" component just mentioned. One pattern of "democratic" leader behavior, as defined by other investigators (100), was also positively related to student self-concept; the pattern of "acceptant transactions, controlling through standards, with appeal to convention as the source of authority, and avoiding negative evaluation." Finally:

> Strong support was found . . . for positive relationships between pupil self-concepts and teacher behavior characterized by a *high degree* of private or semiprivate communication with children, of overt facilitation of task-oriented behavior, of concern for divergent responses in children, of attentiveness to pupil needs, of the use of control techniques involving humor — and a relatively *low degree* of

negative evaluation, of domination through threat, of firmness in tone, of teacher-supportive control, of harsh "taskmaster" behavior, and of grim domination. (160)

The second study, by Peck et al., involved an examination of teacher effects on student achievement and self-esteem (129). Fifty-three sixth grade teachers and their students participated. One aspect of the study focused on the relationships between teacher classroom behavior and student self-esteem. Students completed a self-concept questionnaire in which teachers, based upon classroom observations, were rated on three factors. The three were those found by an earlier researcher to characterize outstanding teachers: (1) *Kindly-Understanding* — friendly, understanding, sympathetic behavior vs. aloof, egocentric behavior; (2) *Systematic-Organized* — responsible, systematic, businesslike vs. unplanned, slipshod behavior; and (3) *Stimulating-Inventive* — stimulating, imaginative behavior vs. dull, routine behavior (141).

Student self-esteem was reported to be affected by all three of these factors (129). More importantly, the effects differed for students with different self-esteem levels. With respect to stimulating-inventive teacher behavior, the evidence indicated a curvilinear relationship. Students working with teachers who demonstrated either high or low stimulating-inventive behavior had higher self-esteem levels at the end of the school year than those working with teachers who showed average stimulating-inventive behavior.

Kindly-understanding teacher behavior was directly related to changes in self-esteem for students who exhibited average or high self-esteem in the fall, but there was an *inverse* relationship for changes in self-esteem for students who exhibited low self-esteem initially. A similar pattern was reported for systematic-organized teacher behavior. These findings seem to indicate that children with average or high self-esteem, working with friendly, understanding, and sympathetic teachers, in all likelihood will develop even higher self-esteem; while children exhibiting low self-esteem, working with these same teachers will develop lower self-esteem. This pattern is perplexing and, unquestionably, warrants further exploration. In the interim, these findings may best be viewed with a jaundiced eye.

The two studies just cited have identified a relationship between teacher behavior and student self-concept. Others suggest at least a link between them. Teacher expectancies influence their behavior. One study reported that teachers gave more verbal feedback to students who were expected to achieve (158); another found that teachers spent more time interacting and gaining feedback from high achievers than from low achievers and students expected to be low achievers (23). In addition, teachers were reported to wait a longer period of time for answers from high achievers than from low achievers (139). Given the known relationship between achievement and self-concept, and the Spaulding and Peck et al. studies just described (160, 129), it is not surprising to find teacher expectations related to student self-concept. However, the evidence is far from conclusive. This becomes more apparent in the literature dealing with sex and self-concept.

Because teachers interact differently with male and female students, we could expect to find a difference in male and female student self-concept. Males generally do receive more attention than females do from teachers; and when the teacher is female this can result in lower self-concepts for females (58). On the other hand, females more than males generally perceive teachers' feelings toward them as being positive (144). Furthermore, it is uncertain if a difference in male and female self-concepts exists. Several researchers report higher self-concept for females than males (11, 54, 7). One researcher, however, discovered the opposite — that is, higher self-concepts for males rather than females (113). Thus, it is unclear if student sex is related to self-concept.

A similar lack of clarity exists in the case of student socioeconomic status (SES) and self-concept. High SES tends to be positively correlated with high self-esteem. One study noted that fifth grade students from higher social classes showed fewer indications of maladjustment (26); another, involving a large sample of elementary school students, reported that students with higher SES showed better adjustment than those with lower SES (151). With regard to middle SES, several investigators maintain the relationship still exists; that is, middle SES students possess higher self-concept than lower SES students (33, 143, 171). But several researchers indicate that by some criteria, low SES students may have more positive self-concepts than middle SES students (170, 171, 186).

Trowbridge tested over thirty-seven hundred third through seventh grade low and middle SES students using Coopersmith's Self-Esteem Inventory (CSEI) (171). The CSEI was selected because it measures four dimensions: (1) general self, (2) social self-peers, (3) home-parents, and (4) school-academic. It has been hypothesized that the cases where lower SES students appear to have higher self-concepts than middle SES students can be attributed to the fact that researchers used a general self-concept measurement rather than an academic self-concept measurement. Trowbridge's findings indicated that the self-concept of the low SES students was significantly higher than those of middle SES on three CSEI dimensions: (1) general self, (2) social self-peers, and (3) school-academic. Only on the home-parent did the middle SES students score higher. Of particular interest are the results for the school-academic dimension. Table 1 presents the results for seven scale items which measure that dimension. Notice that "I'm doing the best work I can" is the only positive item on which middle SES score higher.

TABLE 1

PERCENT OF "LIKE ME" RESPONSES ON CSEI SCHOOL-ACADEMIC SUBSCALE

	Percent of Students Responding "Like Me"	
	Low SES	Middle SES
I like to be called on in class	77.5%	34.8%
I'm not doing as well in school as I'd like to	21.7	59.3
I find it very hard to talk in front of the class	11.3	39.7
I'm proud of my school work	68.3	46.4
I often feel upset in school	6.5	19.1
My teacher makes me feel I'm not good enough	29.7	39.8
*I'm doing the best work I can	6.1	44.5

SOURCE: N. T. Trowbridge. "Self-Concept and Socio-Economic Status in Elementary School Children." *American Educational Research Journal* 9, no. 4 (1972):533. Copyright 1972, American Educational Research Association, Washington, D.C.

Trowbridge offers three explanations for the findings. First, lower SES students may have lower aspiration levels and consequently derive greater satisfaction from their performances. Second, lower SES students may not blame themselves for bad experiences, while middle SES students may view their shortcomings as being their fault. Third, by answering "Not Like Me" to the statement "I'm doing the best work I can," lower SES students are protecting their self-concepts. When students perceive that they are doing their best work and the teacher judges the work as poor, this has a negative effect on self-concept. If, on the other hand, a lower perception is held, the child can better accept failure.

The research findings with respect to the relationship between enthnicity and student self-concept are, at best, mixed and inconclusive (184). For example, one study reported that the self-concept of middle SES Chicanos was similar to that of low SES Anglo children (103); another found no significant differences between the self-concept of Chicanos and Anglos (46). A third found Puerto Rican students' self-concept to be significantly lower than that of Blacks and Anglos (34); but still another reported mixed results (185). One researcher found American Indian students' self-concept significantly lower than that of Anglos (34), while another reported no significant differences (178). For Blacks, the findings are even more equivocal. Several reseachers note differences in the self-concept levels of Blacks and Anglos in favor of Anglos (47, 95, 105), while others report no significant differences (179, 182, 185). Still others report cases where the self-concept of Blacks surpasses that of Anglos. (46, 186). The same mixture of results can be found in studies of the effects of segregated and desegregated school settings on Black student self-concept; some favor a segregated setting (82, 86) and others a desegregated one (79, 185, 186).

The mixed findings may be attributed to many factors, not the least of which is confusion over definitions. Many different operational definitions were utilized in the studies just cited, and consequently different dimensions of the general self-concept have been measured in different studies. Again, several individuals attribute the findings, particularly those in which higher self-concepts were reported for Blacks than for Anglos, to incidences where general self-concept rather than academic self-concept was being measured. However, certain studies report higher self-concept for Blacks even on measures of academic self-concepts (21, 85, 170, 171). One of these (21) explains this phenomenon in terms of reference groups; that is, students in predominantly Black schools assess their academic ability in a context different from that of students in majority Anglo schools. Black students do not base their self-evaluation on middle-class Anglo standards but rather on standards reflected by family, peers, and teachers in school and social systems that are predominantly Black. Notwithstanding this explanation, the overall picture in terms of the relationship between ethnicity and student self-concept is still fuzzy and requires finer tuning through additional research.

Before leaving the topic of ethnicity and self-concept, one further note concerns the differing effects teaching behaviors may have on ethnic membership. The Peck et al. study reported earlier described the relationships between three teaching factors and student self-esteem (129). It was noted that the factors were related differently depending upon the initial self-esteem level of the student. This finding, in the case of two of the three factors, also holds for student ethnicity. Teachers exhibiting high levels of kindly-understanding behavior had a negative effect on the self-esteem of Blacks, while medium levels of the same type behavior had a more positive effect. Among Anglos the medium levels also showed positive effects. For Chicanos, however, the reverse was true. There was a direct relationship in which high levels of kindly-understanding behaviors produced the most positive effects. Different levels of stimulating-inventive teaching behavior were directly related to the self-esteem levels of Anglo students; and for Chicanos, higher levels of stimulating-inventive behavior were related to more positive self-esteem levels on the part of the students. But for Blacks, high levels of this teacher behavior affected them in an adverse manner while medium levels appeared to be most effective in enhancing self-esteem.

Turning our attention to schooling practices, let us first look briefly at the impact of grouping patterns on student self-concept. One pattern is to establish homogeneous and heterogeneous groups based on some criterion of ability or achievement. One study found that heterogeneous grouping was related to improvements in self-concept (92); another reported improved attitudes toward school and school work for this pattern of grouping (145). A third study, on the other hand, reported that self-esteem levels were related to achievement tracking (104). Eighth grade students in Track I, the highest achieving group, scored significantly higher on a self-esteem inventory than students in other tracks, and students in the lowest achieving group, Track IV, scored significantly lower than students in the other three tracks. For multi-age group patterns the evidence is still rather skimpy, but some can be found favoring this pattern (80).

The practice of nonpromotion of academically deficient students has a long history of debate in educational circles. Several educators have theorized that nonpromotion would have grave psychological effects on the child, and some empirical evidence exists to support this claim. Three studies report that both single and multiple nonpromotions have a negative effect on the self-concept of students (91, 17, 175). However, these investigations contained at least one major flaw. Data on self-concept levels were not collected prior to nonpromotion. Two investigators who collected this pretest information found that nonpromotion did not adversely affect self-concept development (32, 65). In fact, just the opposite appeared to be the case. For example, one found that the self-concept levels of promoted and nonpromoted students were very similar after one year (65). He tested the two primary grade student groups at four intervals: fall and spring of grade one and fall and spring of grade two. Differences between the mean self-concept levels of the groups in the fall of the first year were noticeable, but by the spring of the second year, mean self-concept scores for the two groups were almost identical. Thus, although the effects of nonpromotion on student self-concept remain unclear, some evidence reveals no adverse effects and the possibility of positive effects.

A schooling practice that is receiving a great deal of attention today is mainstreaming. With the passage of P.L. 94-142 and state mandates, the education of handicapped students is once again in the limelight. The legislation requires the placement of these students in the "least restrictive" environment. Ostensively at least, this suggests the placement of some handicapped children in so-called "regular" classrooms, in the mainstream of instructional settings. As a result of the legislation, there has been a rekindling of the debate of the benefits of "special" vs. "regular" class placements. Some feel that special class settings will more appropriately meet the academic and psychological needs of special students while others believe that the ability, achivement, and social mix found in the "regular" classroom is appropriate to meet the needs of all students. With respect to the question of effects on self-concept development, the empirical evidence appears to support both views. Some studies report lower self-concepts for handicapped students placed in "special" classrooms (15, 111); some report the opposite (49, 8); others report no significant difference (108, 172). Several reasons can be cited for this conflicting evidence. First, the studies deal with different populations of handicapped students and differing definitions of the term "handicapped." Second, different dimensions of self-concept are often being measured. Third, existing self-concept instruments may not be appropriate to use with particular special students. Fourth, it may be too early to accurately assess the impact of "regular" vs. "special" class placement of handicapped children.

This fourth reason is of particular importance in the light of present knowledge. We know that teachers' attitudes and perceptions affect their interactions with students (23). We also know that some teachers hold negative attitudes toward "special" students and that, in many cases, these attitudes reflect a lack of knowledge and understanding of handicapped individuals. Evidence suggests that a majority of "regular" classroom teachers are ill prepared to work with "handicapped" students (88).

Additionally, and more importantly, we know that improved preparation, either at the pre-service or in-service level, can lead to improved attitudes and the acquisition of the skills needed to work with special students (88). Preparation of this type is still in the beginning stages of development and not yet widespread. Additional time will need to pass before we can determine the impact of mainstreaming on student self-concept. Until the newly prepared teachers have had ample opportunity to impact their school settings, the jury must remain out.

The relationship between the "open classroom" and student self-concept has also received renewed attention in recent years. If, as it has been suggested, we accept the Progressive Education Movement of the 1930s as representing the beginnings of the open classroom movement, then we may say that developing "openness" in school settings has a relatively long history. It may be more appropriate, however, to assign the beginnings to the mid-1960s — the period in which American educators began to learn about the English open primary schools. What followed was a swing of the educational pendulum in the direction of more openness in educational settings. The swing may be attributed to many factors, not the least of which was changing social conditions. But the most convincing educational claims were that openness promoted more "humane" learning, achievement gains equal to or greater than those found in traditional settings, and, just as important, substantial improvements in student attitudes and self-images. The extensive Bank Street College of Education study (117) lends a great deal of support to these claims. In studying fourth graders from four New York City schools, the investigators found essentially no significant difference in achievement scores for students in the traditional and modern schools. On the other hand, they did find differences in student self-concepts, in favor of the more modern schools. Students in these schools were less rigid, more cooperative, and exhibited more positive attitudes toward school.

More recent studies reveal mixed results. For example, some investigators report more positive self-concepts for students enrolled in open classroom or open space settings (99, 25, 9). Others, however, report lower self-concepts (142, 106). Horwitz, after reviewing 61 selected studies, reported that 25 percent favored open classrooms, 3 percent favored traditional settings, 25 percent showed mixed results, and 47 percent showed no significant differences (89).

Why has the evidence proved inconclusive? One reason may be that academic achievement is an intervening variable; that is, the discrepancies may be explained in terms of achievement, and achievement gains are a stronger determinant of self-concept gains than the type of setting. Horwitz's findings may be said to give some credence to this explanation. Although unscientific, a review of his findings shows that the studies of the relationship between achievement and open classroom settings follow a pattern similar to that of self-concept. Fourteen percent of the studies favor the open classroom as enhancing achievement, 12 percent favor traditional settings, 28 percent show mixed results, and 46 percent report no significant differences. More conclusive support of this explanation is found in the 1977 Abt Associates report, the source of the following excerpt.

> 1. Highly structured basic skills programs were much more successful than "open classroom" approaches in raising the achievement level of low income children.
> 2. Open classrooms generally failed to raise self-esteem, even though that was a primary objective . . . [structured programs] with a primary objective of teaching basic skills [were] more effective in raising self-esteem.(90)

A second reason for the problematic findings may be the definition and measurement of self-concept. Horwitz reports that almost all the studies define self-concept as a single dimensional variable — they measure only one component of self-concept such as academic self-concept or self-esteem. Evidence which may reveal the weakness of defining self-concept in such a fashion can be found in a study of primary grade students in open and traditional classrooms who were tested for achievement and self-concept levels (87). No significant differences were found between the groups for achievement and academic self-concept, but significant differences were found, in favor of the open classroom students, for global self-concept.

Finally, there is a great deal of confusion over the definition of open classroom. The term is often erroneously equated with open space or other "openness" settings and approaches. As Horwitz states:

> Silberman (1970) has characterized "openness" as "less an approach or method than a set of shared attitudes and convictions about the nature of childhood, learning, and schooling." (p. 208). Yet some writers who describe open classrooms are clearly more concerned with physical space than with attitudes or convictions. To them, the term open has primarily an *architectural* meaning, and open classrooms are simply large, *open* rooms with many children and not many walls. What goes on pedagogically in these open spaces may or may not be the same thing as open education. . . . (89)

Teachers untrained to work in open classrooms may find the approach inconsistent with their style of teaching. The result, many times, may be the creation of physical and psychological barriers to "openness" such as those described by Silberman (155) and Horwitz (89).

To summarize this entire section, then, we have observed that in general student self-concept becomes more negative through the schooling years. There is considerable evidence that indicates a direct relationship between achievement and self-concept; that is, higher achievement is accompanied by higher self-concept and low achievement by low self-concept. Teacher characteristics are also related to self-concept development. Teachers' self-image, their interactions with students, and their teaching styles all relate to student self-concept. Furthermore, these teacher characteristics may have a different impact on self-concept depending upon the ethnicity of the student. It is unclear if, and, in some cases, how, the student's sex, socioeconomic status, or ethnic background influences his/her self-concept. With respect to specific schooling practices, it remains unclear how grouping patterns, mainstreaming, and open classroom settings are related to student self-concept. The impact of nonpromotion practices is also open to question, but recent studies report no adverse effects and apparently some positive effects on self-concept. Thus, as one would expect, schooling practices are related to self-concept development, but additional research is needed before their impact can be fully understood.

The Impact of Self-Concept Enhancement Strategies

The preceding section has described what is known about the relationships between certain schooling variables and student self-concept. It discussed the possible impact of the normal everyday activities of formal schooling on self-concept development. Additionally, it indicated that an activity may interact differently with the self-concepts of different students — a particular activity appears to improve the self-concept of some students while it is detrimental to others. The task then becomes one of identifying ways to improve those self-concepts that for a variety of reasons have become psychologically damaged. More importantly, the task becomes one of identifying strategies and activities that will effectively enhance the self-concepts of *all* students. Before turning to a discussion of these strategies, it is important to highlight the general problems that may be encountered in attempts to change self-concept.

How can teachers best help students to change their self-concepts? A psychologist and therapist says that he is tempted to answer this question in one of two ways. First:

> You can't! There's no way you can reach into someone else's psyche and rearrange their self-perceptions. The real issues are what do *they* have to do in order to perceive themselves differently and how can you help them to define and implement those steps? (68)

And alternatively:

> Don't try to change it! The more you can understand people as they are and accept, value and respect them, then the more they *and* their self-concepts will change. (68)

Neither of these answers is very satisfying, which Fitts acknowledges by stating, "They are too vague and general, not operational enough, and actually extremely difficult to carry out . . ." (68). Furthermore, for educators, such responses are unacceptable. Educators are charged with promoting the psychological development of children, but these answers leave too much to chance. We must therefore search for more systematic and exacting methods of influencing self-concept development.

Recognizing the task and accepting the challenge, however, does not make the task any easier, as will be seen in subsequent pages. It is difficult for many reasons, not the least of which is the problem of accurately and empirically measuring self-concept change. This problem may become clearer by examining a hypothetical situation.

Suppose we identify a strategy which we believe will enhance the self-concepts of our students and we set out in a systematic manner to test the hypothesis. We administer a pretest, some measure of self-concept; we implement the strategy for a period of time; and we administer a self-concept post-test. Upon analyzing the data we find no significant change; that is, we find no significant gains in student self-concept. Apparently the strategy was not effective in enhancing the self-concept of the students. Or was it? Are there alternative explanations for these findings? If so, what are they? First, what have we measured — general self-concept or some dimension of general self-concept? We may have been unclear as to what we desired to measure and, consequently, selected an inappropriate self-concept scale. Related to the selection of the appropriate self-concept instrument is the matter of the validity and reliability of the instrument. Some scales are valid and reliable only for certain populations, certain ages. Also, few scales are valid for use with very young children. So, a second explanation may be that the instrument selected may not validly measure the self-concepts of the student age group.

Third, self-concept scales are generally self-reporting instruments. Students report their perceptions of their self-concepts. They represent "what a person is willing, able or can be seduced to say about self" (36). And further:

> Too many other variables intervene between self-concept and the self-report to modify or distort what the person is able or willing to say about self. Just a few of these variables may be: the willingness of the subject to cooperate, the subject's possession of adequate language to express his experiential self, social expectancies impinging upon the subject at the time he or she is asked for self descriptions, the subject's own goals or purposes in the encounter, the relationship with the requester, and the subject's freedom from threat or coercion — [these] are only a few of the possible sources of error. (36)

So, our findings may be explained by the fact that the use of a self-reporting instrument distorted the true self-concepts or changes in self-concepts of our students.

Fourth, the self-concept scores reflect *group* self-concepts, not *individual* self-concepts. We have obtained average self-concept scores for the total group, but we have not looked at individual self-concept scores. Our intervention strategy undoubtedly affected students differently. The strategy may have enhanced the self-concept of some students, affected others in a negative fashion, and had no impact on others. These different effects may average out, when grouped together, to no effect. Thus, the strategy may be beneficial for some students, but this benefit is not visible in the analysis of group data.

Finally, how long does it take before the strategy has an impact on students' self-concepts and how long before it becomes empirically identifiable? Possibly the strategy is a good one, but it was not employed for a sufficient period of time to have an impact and for the impact to be observable. As indicated previously, general self-concept becomes embedded early in life. Fortunately or unfortunately, depending upon the case, it becomes resistant to change. The results of the hypothetical study may merely reflect this resistance and indicate that continued use of the strategy may prove beneficial.

It is important to be aware of these alternative explanations of these findings. Awareness should not, however, discourage our efforts. These explanations are presented here as cautionary notes to consider during the quest to identify effective means to enhance our students' self-concepts. Keeping them in mind, let us now return our attention to an analysis of the empirical findings.

What strategies should we employ to improve the self-concepts of our students? First, consider the evidence regarding academic achievement and self-concept. As noted earlier, researchers have identified a direct relationship between achievement and self-concept, specifically academic self-concept. This state of affairs has led many to theorize about a causal relationship between the two variables. As a result theorists have joined one of two camps. One group, the self-enhancement theorists, believes that self-concept explains achievement. Their argument is that changes in self-concept cause changes in achievement. Therefore, an improvement in the student's self-concept will in turn cause an improvement in the student's achievement. The second school of thought, the skill development theorists, believes the opposite to be the case. Achievement explains self-concept — changes in self-concept are caused by, or result from, initial changes in achievement. Consequently, these theorists urge us to identify methods for improving a student's academic achievement because such achievement will then enhance the student's self-concept.

Recent investigations give greater credence to the skill development school of thought. The Kifer study, for instance, adds graphic support to this approach to enhancing self-concept (96). In a cross-sectional study, Kifer examined the long-term effects of multiple academic successes and failures. Students in the upper fifth and lowest fifth of their class, in terms of teacher marks, were examined over four time periods: grades 1–2, grades 1–4, grades 1–6, and grades 1–8. In other words, one group of students ranked in the upper fifth and another group in the lowest fifth of their class for two years (grades 1–2), other groups for four years (grades 1–4), and so forth. Essentially, then, some students had two years of success or failure, and others had four, six, or eight years of success or failure. Each group of students was given a modification of Brookover's test of academic self-concept. Kifer's results are presented in Figure 1.

The results clearly show that the academic self-concept of successful and unsuccessful students becomes more different with the passage of time. Kifer interprets these results as support for the theory that changes in achievement cause changes in self-concept; and Bloom, after cautioning us,

FIGURE 1

ACADEMIC SELF-CONCEPT MEAN SCORES FOR SUCCESSFUL AND UNSUCCESSFUL STUDENTS

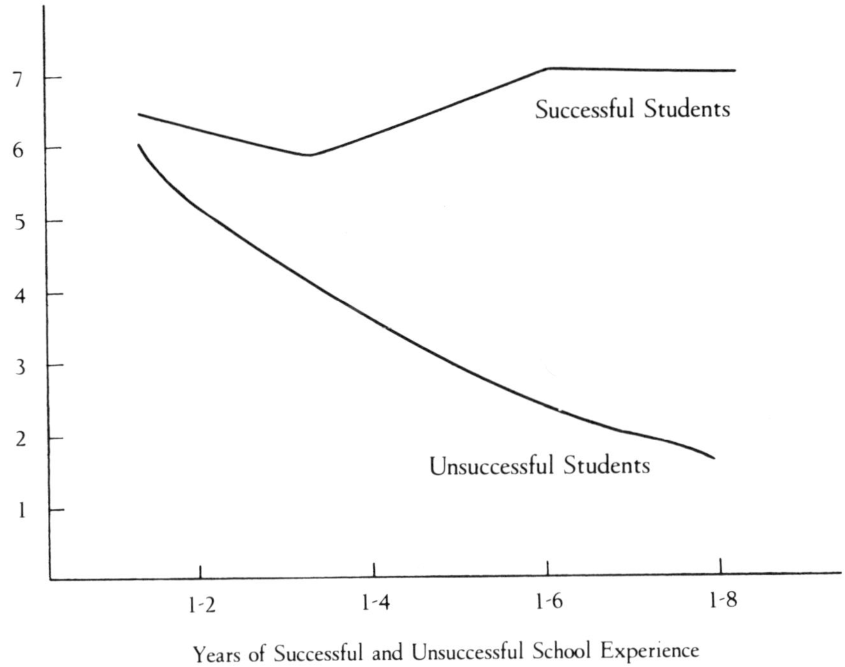

SOURCE: Edward Kifer, "The Effects of School Achievement on the Affective Traits of the Learner," paper presented at the Annual Conference of the American Educational Research Association, New Orleans, 1973. Copyright © 1973. Printed with permission.

states ". . . the evidence provided by this study strongly implies that self-concept of ability is in large part dependent on students' perceptions of their relative achievement (teachers' marks) over these critical years in the elementary-junior high school period" (14).

Other researchers (29) came to a similar conclusion after reanalyzing the data of a longitudinal study conducted by Brookover and his associates. Using a specialized statistical technique called cross-lagged panel correlation, they performed a secondary analysis of self-concept of ability scores for over 550 eighth through twelfth graders and concluded:

> The results are clearly more supportive of a skill development model in which academic achievement is causally

> predominant over self-concept of ability as well as perceived evaluation of others, rather than a two-stage self-enhancement model in which perceived evaluation of others is causally predominant over self-concept of ability, which in turn is causally predominant over academic achievement. Apparently, adolescents' performance in school more often affects their self-concept of ability and their perception of others' assessment of ability leads to changes in self-concept of ability, which in turn leads to changes in academic performance. (29)

Further evidence in support of the skill development model can be found in three additional studies. Researchers working with seventh graders reported that students who were told that they failed an academic test tended to regard themselves less highly than others (74). Another investigator, using a similar methodology told half the members of a group that they had scored high on a self-concept test and the other half that they had scored low (130). Scores on a subsequent personality scale revealed that subjects who had been given a high test score rated themselves significantly higher on selected personality traits than those who had been given a low score. Although an achievement test was not used in this study, it is fairly safe to hypothesize that because a rating of high or low was assigned to the test results, the subjects reacted as they would to an academic exercise. The third study used a mathematics test to explore the effects of induced academic failure on self-concept (28). After being administered a mathematics test and one-half of a self-concept test, third graders were assigned to one of two groups. Students in the first group were told they scored very well on the mathematics test; those in the second group were told they did poorly. Both groups were then given the second half of the self-concept test. The results showed that the self-concept scores of the first group — students who were told they did well — did not change, but the scores for the second group — students who were told they did poorly — decreased.

Finally, additional support for the skill development model is evident in the work of two investigators who conducted a fairly extensive review of programs and strategies designed to improve achievement by first enhancing self-concept (147). Many of the programs reviewed were the federally funded intervention programs in compensatory education, such as Head Start, Follow Through, and Upward Bound. These researchers report that their evaluation of the intervention programs generally failed to find a causal relationship between self-concept changes and achievement and, after exploring alternative explanations, they concluded that the evidence favors the skill development model.

These recent findings suggest that as we identify more effective ways of improving the academic achievement of our students, we will promote the enhancement of their self-concepts. Such evidence, however, does not imply that this strategy is the only one to be employed to enhance student self-concept. The studies just described focus only upon academic self-concept. Other dimensions of the general self-concept are equally important and deserve attention. And, clearly, the evidence does not rule out the value of the self-enhancement model. Undoubtedly, a two-way street operates between achievement and self-concept. Achievement leads to higher self-concept and, in turn, higher self-concept leads to greater achievement. In addition, a student's self-concept influences his/her motivation to learn in the first place (6). If students do not feel good about themselves generally and good about themselves specifically as learners, they will lack the motivation to improve their performance in many school-related activities. Therefore, it is important to identify a multitude of ways to enhance our students' general self-concepts.

What additional strategies can be gleaned from the research literature? One cluster of variables involves teacher behavior. As noted earlier, Spaulding reported positive relationships between "socially-integrative" and "learner-supportive" teacher behaviors and student self-concept (160). These behaviors included calm, accepting behavior, attention to the learning task, and attentiveness to student needs.

Poris hypothesized that there was a relationship between ATB's (affective teacher behaviors) and student self-concept and divergent production (132). She defined ATB's as (1) involvement of students in goal setting; (2) use of positive statements regarding students and the avoidance of threat; (3) facilitation of values clarification; and experiences whereby students can (4) experiment and evaluate; and (5) give and receive helpful feedback to and from each other. Working with teachers of third through sixth grade, Poris found partial support for all her hypotheses except peer feedback. This study coupled with Spaulding's findings thus indicates that as teachers develop or improve upon these specific types of behaviors, they can anticipate improvement in student self-concept.

Teacher encouragement of self-evaluation and reinforcement is another stratey that merits attention. The Felker study reports that students with high self-concepts tend to make positive statements to themselves after performing school tasks (63). It was hypothesized that if students could be taught to evaluate and reinforce themselves positively, they would develop more positive self-concepts. To this end, the researchers designed a training program to help teachers learn how to encourage self-evaluation and reinforcement. The training was divided into five components, each designed to promote development of a specific strategy: (1) Adults, Praise Yourselves; (2) Teach Children to Praise Themselves; (3) Teach Children to Praise Others; (4) Teach Children to Set Realistic Goals; and (5) Help Children Evaluate Realistically. The researchers report that students, taught by teachers trained in the five components, developed higher self-concepts and experienced less anxiety and fewer failures. A more recent study reveals that the two most effective components for enhancing self-concept are teacher self-praise and student praise of others (16).

Tutoring programs in which students tutor other students are often proposed as a strategy for improving achievement and self-concept. The empirical evidence presents a mixed picture of the outcomes of such programs. Some programs purport to increase the achievement of the tutor, some the tutee, and some both. The same holds true in the case of affective outcomes, and, specifically, self-concept. The mixed results have been attributed by certain researchers to the use of unscientific research methodologies and the disregard for theoretical issues. These researchers state, "Unless investigators in this area make a stronger attempt to draw more directly upon the mainstream of psychological and educational theory, it is likely that tutoring research will continue to be rather fragmented, inconclusive, and noncumulative" (2). Nevertheless, descriptions of a few exemplary programs warrant attention here.

Drawing upon the Lippitt and Lippitt cross-age tutoring model, the Ontario-Montclair School District in California implemented a three-year program in which seventh and eighth graders tutored low-achieving fourth through sixth grade students in reading, mathematics, and language arts (125). Tutoring involved 35-45 minute sessions, three times a week. Results indicated that both tutors and tutees made academic gains, but neither group showed significant self-concept improvement. Similar findings were reported for a four-month compensatory program in which eighth through twelfth grade volunteers worked with low-achieving second through fifth grade students (120). Tutors and tutees made significant academic gains over a control group, but neither group showed increased self-concept scores.

The results of a study in which third and fourth grade students tutored first and second graders in reading indicated that tutees, working with the tutors who had received specific reading instruction, showed greater gains in reading and self-concept scores (70). Another study focused on reading achievement and self-concept of second through fourth graders tutored on a one-to-one basis by undergraduate education majors (162). Its results indicated that, after ten weeks of instruction, tutees had not made significant gains in reading, but had improved their self-concept in some areas. Neither of these two investigations reports self-concept gains for the tutors. Evaluations of the Youth Tutoring Youth (YTY) program, on the other hand, report positive self-concept gains for both tutees and tutors (123). The YTY program is designed to benefit academically disadvantaged elementary and secondary school students, and the evaluation reveals that participation in the program improved the reading skills and self-concepts of both tutors and tutees.

Finally, two studies report self-concept gains for the tutor. The first study investigated the effect of being a tutor on attitudes (181). One group of low-achieving fifth and sixth graders received training and then tutored a group of first grade students. A second group received training but did not tutor, and a third group neither trained nor participated in tutoring experiences. Results showed that tutors who were trained and subsequently tutored first graders had significantly more positive attitudes toward self and school than either of the control groups. Similar results were reported in a study focusing on the unmotivated student (119). Poorly motivated students selected to tutor younger unmotivated peers showed improved motivation, self-concepts, and achievement as a result of the program.

These few examples suggest that the self-concepts of either the tutor or tutee may be improved by cross-age tutoring programs. However, a cautionary note is in order. A like number of studies can be identified in which no self-concept gains were found for either participant. Therefore, additional research is necessary before more exacting conclusions can be formulated regarding the effects of peer-tutoring. The lack of negative findings, however, suggests that tutoring programs *may* warrant attention as a means for enhancing student self-concept.

Many strategies may have been developed specifically for self-concept enhancement. The underlying premises of these strategies are that attempts to improve self-concept necessitate infusing into the curriculum activities purposely created with this goal in mind. An interesting, but unfortunately unsuccessful, strategy involved teaching students skills that were believed to be valued by their peers (97). The researcher hypothesized that special recognition by peers would result in improved self-concepts.

Students were taught magic tricks that could be demonstrated to their peers. Analysis of the results revealed no significant difference or gains in self-concept scores for students who acquired the magic skills.

A much more elaborate self-concept enhancement strategy was utilized with groups of third, fourth, and fifth grade students (163). This study concluded that because a multitude of factors interact and influence a child's self-concept, a variety of effective strategies should be used in the classroom. To this end, the researchers developed three model strategy programs. The first involved an entire class in which a subgroup of low self-concept students had been identified. The second focused on giving special attention to a subgroup of low self-concept students within a classroom. The third matched a subgroup of low self-concept students with a similar group of high self-concept peers.

Group One created Happiness Books, containing positive statements by others. Each day students and teacher drew names and then entered a positive statement in the Happiness Book concerning the person whose name they had drawn. In Group Two, the subgroup was targeted for increased positive feedback; and in Group Three, the matched subgroup participated in one-hour group games such as "thumb wrestling" and "cooperative squares." Results of the six-week study indicated that Group One, the total class strategy, was most effective in improving self-concepts. In fact, the self-concept scores improved for all students, lows and highs. The results also showed that some students may need specialized help. It appears, then, that all three strategies may be important and useful in improving student self-concept.

A strategy often proposed as a means to increased affective outcomes is that of self-expression. The theory is that various forms of self-expression will give students opportunities to reevaluate themselves and to gain greater self-confidence in their abilities. For instance, puppetry is believed to improve a child's self-concept (31); and the use of dance as such a medium has been supported (173). Studies evaluating these strategies have reported mixed results, with a majority reporting no significant self-concept gains. The same holds true for other strategies. A creative dramatics program did not show gains for secondary school students (127); but improved self-concept was reported for second and fifth graders who participated in creative drama exercises (52). One researcher suggests that a media program in which students have an opportunity to develop their own videotape production enhances self-concept development (126); while others report that a photographic enhancement program did not result in significant gains in self-esteem scores (3). Thus, these results indicate a lack of consensus on the value of self-expression strategies. But they do not rule out their potential benefit, for in many cases the studies lack desired levels of scientific objectivity, and results are based on brief treatment periods.

One strategy found to be effective in modifying behavior and improving student self-concept is based on the postulate that if students had an opportunity to view and examine their own behavior and that of others, they would change their behavior in a positive direction (71). Using videotape, fourth through sixth grade students were encouraged to analyze classroom behavior and patterns of interaction. It was found that the analysis led to positive changes in self-concept, with the greatest gains in students who were not videotaped themselves, but who participated in the viewing and analysis of the behavior of peers.

In recent years, several commercially packaged affective education programs have been marketed for use in the classroom, among which are (1) the Human Development Program; (2) Developing Understanding of Self and Others; and (3) Dimensions of Personality. Each of these three programs has received considerable use in the classroom and a fair amount of evaluation. After reviewing each of them, researchers concluded that these programs have shown mixed results regarding enhancement of student self-concept (116).

Known by many as "Magic Circle," the Human Development Program (HDP) was developed by Bessell and Palomares (12). This program of materials and exercises is designed to improve student interpersonal communications. Three of its objectives have been identified as follows: "to help children to: (a) understand the similarities and differences between themselves and others, (b) identify and properly use their own abilities, and (c) recognize their role in social relationships" (116).

Two studies report no significant improvement in self-concept for fourth graders (56), and for second, fourth, and sixth grade students (45), who had participated in HDP. Other investigators report that in a study using HDP with grades one through three, the program did not improve the self-esteem of students, and in fact the self-esteem of a control group, students not exposed to HDP, increased more than the experimental group (116). Another study involved three groups: one group used HDP for thirteen weeks, a second group used it for twenty-five weeks, and a third group did not use it (122). Results showed no significant differences in the self-esteem scores of the first and third groups. Significant gains were found for the second group. Other studies reported that groups using HDP for a relatively short period of time did not show significant self-esteem gains, but groups using HDP or alternative affective education programs for longer periods of time did show significant gains in self-esteem scores (164, 43).

Dinkmeyer's Developing Understanding of Self and Others (DUSO) (48) is designed to help young children understand the consequences of their behavior and teach self-acceptance, decisionmaking, and social responsibility. The program consists of materials such as storybooks, records, puppetry materials, and role-playing cards to be used by students in problem situation cases. The purpose of the activities, according to their developer, is "to help the child become more aware of the relationships between himself, other people, and his needs and goals" (48). In terms of empirical evidence, DUSO was reported not effective in improving the self-concepts of fourth graders (133); and similar findings were reported for second graders and first through third grade students respectively (140, 112). However, one study reported that DUSO was effective in increasing the social awareness of first graders (66), and another reported improved self-images for primary grade students (183). Thus, additional research is needed in order to determine with any assurance if DUSO is effective in enhancing students' self-concepts.

The third program, Limbacher's Dimensions of Personality (DOP), is designed to help students understand their motives and emotions (102). This curriculum packet of materials has been described as designed "to promote confidence, competence, cooperation, self-awareness, self-understanding, and self-acceptance" (116). Activities include reading passages and group discussions, and the teacher serves as facilitator as the students explore their feelings and opinions. Little empirical evidence on the effectiveness of the program has been reported, but the available data appears to support the effectiveness of the program (116).

Group counseling as a means to self-concept improvement is also a strategy that has been employed with increased frequency in recent years. Generally, this type of counseling is viewed as effective in helping students explore their thoughts and emotions and thereby develop more realistic self-images. For example, in a group counseling program developed for fourth and fifth graders, the sessions focused on student concerns and interests (128). The counselors were encouraged to create a supportive environment in which students would feel free to share perceptions and emotions. Data collected at the end of the program revealed that the participating students showed greatest gains in the area of interpersonal relationships and gains on some self-concept dimensions. Another study involved two group counseling models for working with low self-concept elementary school students (51). One was a verbal model and the other a play media model. Results showed that the play media model was superior in improving students' self-concepts.

With regard to high school age students, a nondirective group counseling program was reported effective in helping students gain in acceptance of self and others (18). The group counseling model was also found to be effective in improving student self-concept, in a study that concluded that the amount of improvement depends upon group congruence: "If a student perceived the other group members, including the counselor, to be genuine, accepting, and understanding, he has a better chance for personal growth than if he were in a group offering a poorer relationship" (81). Therefore, to be effective the composition of the group should be taken into consideration when designing group counseling programs.

Finally, a strategy which is beginning to attract the interest of educators is the development of a parent-teacher partnership. As noted earlier, parents continue to be viewed as "significant others" long into the formal schooling years. It is logical to assume then that efforts directed at helping parents improve their children's self-concepts should aid teachers in similar efforts in the classroom. Unfortunately, there is at present far too little evidence to validate this strategy. The most significant study was conducted over a decade ago when Brookover and his associate tested three different strategies for enhancing academic self-concept (20). Working with approximately 50 low-achieving ninth graders, these researchers developed three types of experimental programs to impact the students' self-concept and achievement. One method involved working with parents, a second with a counselor, and the third with a university "expert." The counselor and expert attempted to convey enhancing information directly to their student groups, while the parent strategy entailed helping parents raise their achievement expectations and evaluations of their children. The study reported that the parent strategy was the only one of the three which was successful in increasing academic self-concept and achievement. This strategy was described as follows:

> In this experiment the parents were told not to reward or reinforce any negative statements their children might make about their academic ability. They were told to avoid even such statements as "Uncle Joe wasn't good in arithmetic either." The children were to

be constantly told in subtle fashion that they were able and ought to be better in school. Any positive statement of ability by the student or any success in school was to be rewarded with commendatory remarks and support. (20)

Brookover suggests a key to the success of the strategy may have been telling parents in the beginning that they were, in part, responsible for their children's low academic self-concepts and that they could be instrumental in changing them. Whatever the key may be, this study demonstrates that parents and teachers can form a partnership which will effectively lead to improved student self-concept. Consequently, its findings should prompt us to begin developing other partnership strategies for working with students.

In sum, this section has revealed that by improving the academic achievement levels of students, we will in all likelihood improve their self-concepts. By creating learner-supportive environments and exhibiting calm, accepting behavior coupled with attention to the learning task, we can expect to see positive gains. In addition, by modeling self-praise and by encouraging students to praise their peers, we facilitate positive self-concept development. Tutoring programs, self-expression activities, and the use of commercially developed affective education programs may also be effective strategies. Group counseling programs, if properly designed, will benefit self-concept; and parent-teacher partnership programs appear to hold great potential for enhancing student self-concept.

THE TEACHER'S ROLE IN SELF-CONCEPT ENHANCEMENT

The preceding sections have considered the literature on self-concept development. We have learned that such development begins very soon after birth, and the early years are crucial to the development of a child's generalized self-concept. We have learned what happens to the child's self-image once he/she begins the formal schooling years, and what generally happens to that child's self-concept as he/she progresses through the school years. We have also looked at the effects of self-concept development strategies on the child. We have learned that certain strategies appear to be effective in changing self-concepts in a positive way. The literature has made it abundantly clear that, after parents, teachers may be the most important "significant others" in the eyes of children. By their actions or inactions, teachers determine in large measure whether a child will leave the schools with a psychologically sound and positive self-concept or one psychologically damaged. Thus, we as teachers play a vital role in determining a child's self-concept. It is important for us to become cognizant of this fact and to consciously search for ways of building positive self-concepts in our students. This section suggests some useful guidelines to employ in working with students, and it briefly describes some of the materials and strategies to use in helping students develop stable, positive self-concepts.

What principles should guide the teacher's actions in working with students? First, "the prevention of negative self-concepts is a vital first step in teaching" (134). We have seen what may happen to a child's self-concept in the school years. It decreases with repeated academic failure and it is influenced by the type of classroom environment we create and project to our students. Also, it is influenced by our perceptions of students and our interactions with them. Correcting these practices would be good first steps, and in so doing we would be building the foundation for more positive actions.

The second and third principles concern teachers' beliefs. We have noted that a teacher's self-concept is related to his/her students' self-concepts. Accordingly, teachers who view themselves in a positive manner will project these images to their students and will provide valuable role models for them. Teachers who have realistic conceptions of themselves, who are accepting of themselves and others, and who accent their positive attributes will help students make realistic assessments and begin to view themselves in a positive light. Furthermore, how the teacher views his/her students will have an impact on the students' self-concept. We know that a student's self-concept is influenced by the student's perception of the teacher's feelings toward him/her, and we have learned that a teacher's expectations are oftentimes transferred to the student. Thus, teachers who view their students in a positive way and project favorable expectations will promote positive self-concept development.

A fourth principle, and possibly the most important one, is that teachers must *plan* for the self-concept development of their students. It cannot be left to chance. We must plan for it just as we plan for the accomplishment of other student outcomes. We must identify ways to assess student self-concept and develop activities to promote self-concept enhancement. In essence, we must diagnose present levels and implement strategies that will lead to more positive outcomes:

> The task of diagnosis and remediation for self-concept enhancement doesn't differ from a teacher's intervention for diagnosing and remediating any weakness found in school. With children who are found to have an overall positive self-concept, there would be a continued fostering of positive self-feelings, just as with children who read well there are more and more challenging books given them to read. The key to any behavioral change, whether it be in the cognitive or in the affective domain, is to diagnose children's specific weaknesses or strengths and then to use appropriate procedures to move them to more adequate levels of functioning. (144)

Keeping these general principles in mind, let us turn to an examination of diagnostic and intervention strategies we can utilize to improve the self-concepts of our students.

Diagnosis of Student Self-Concept

How can we describe a student's self-concept? How can we diagnose this construct called self-concept? Not very easily. By definition, self-concept is private, it is one's private image of oneself. It is based upon self-perception and perceptions of others and it reflects our innermost feelings. We cannot get inside someone's head and heart to see the self, so we must rely on behavior. We must make inferences based upon overt actions. Consequently, we are immediately faced with problems. As noted earlier, for a variety of reasons a person may not wish to project a true self-concept. Also, as observers of behavior we are limited by our perceptions (134,144). We may not be trained observers and may misinterpret actions. And our judgment may reflect our own biases. Biases may influence our attempts at self-perception, and, unless we are aware of them, they are likely to influence our judgments of others. We must be aware of these problems in order not to oversimplify the task. Whenever possible we should seek the help of trained specialists, but realistically we will have to depend on our own observations many times. By recognizing the problem and limitations faced, we place ourselves in a better position to exercise caution and act accordingly.

Given these guidelines, how should we proceed in diagnosing student self-concept? Essentially, two methods are available: observation and self-reporting. With observation we attempt to acquire an objective picture of the student and his/her behavior. What should we include in the picture?

> In observing a person we usually begin with his appearance. We can become aware of the clothes he wears and the way he wears them. We can consider his height and weight, his posture, his grooming, and his general cleanliness. We can take note of any physical problems and his apparent state of health. Next we can take into account his behavior — his speech, his movements, his facial expressions, his manners, his habits, and his reactions. We can be particularly alert to fleeting clues which tell us how he relates to his peer group and to adults, taking into account the things he seeks out and the things he avoids, the way he reacts to success and to failure, to approval and disapproval, and the way he spends his spare time. From all these observations we gather the raw material which we may use to draw inferences. (134)

In addition to this raw material, we can look for the presence or absence of certain qualities. The following six questions may guide our observations.

1. Does the learner make his own decisions (self-directed)?
2. Does the learner feel secure with himself?
3. Does the child have a positive attitude toward learning?
4. Does the child accept himself (race, ethnic)?
5. Is the learner able to deal with his inner conflicts?
6. Does the learner exhibit goal-oriented behavior? (174)

Certain characteristics may aid our observations of young children (166). Table 2 describes these characteristics in terms of a positive and negative self-concept. These characteristics could easily be used as items on an observational checklist which would provide teachers with a more systematic means of developing a profile of individual students. A key point to keep in mind is that the profile would need to be developed over an extended time period. Single observations may reflect unique situations or circumstances; they may not portray an accurate picture of a child's general self-concept.

TABLE 2
CHARACTERISTICS OF POSITIVE AND NEGATIVE GLOBAL SELF-CONCEPTS IN YOUNG CHILDREN

Child with Positive Self-Concept	Child with Negative Self-Concept
Is unafraid of a new situation	Seldom shows initiative
Makes friends with other children easily	Relies on others for direction
Experiments easily with new materials	Seldom enters new activities
Trusts his/her teacher even though he/she is a stranger to him/her	Asks permission to do anything
Is cooperative and can usually follow reasonable rules	Seldom shows spontaneity
Is largely responsible for controlling his/her own behavior	Seldom enters new activities
Is creative, imaginative, and has his/her own ideas	Is possessive of objects
Talks freely and may have difficulty listening to others because of eagerness to share his/her experiences	Talks very little
Is independent and needs only a minimum amount of help or directions from the teacher	Is possessive of objects
Seems for the most part to be a happy individual	Withdraws or aggresses and reacts with signs of frustration

The Florida Key is a learner self-concept scale which may be appropriate for use with students of all ages (135). It is designed to assist teachers in evaluating a student's perception of himself/herself as a learner. The scale is composed of questions which assess four dimensions: (1) Relating, (2) Asserting, (3) Investing, and (4) Coping. Through observation and inference, teachers rate the student on each question along a continuum from *never* to *very often*. The rating is determined by asking the following questions:

Compared with other students of the same age, does this student:

1. get along with other students?
2. get along with the teachers?
3. keep calm when things go wrong?
4. say good things about his/her school?
5. tell the truth about his/her school work?

6. speak up for his/her own ideas?
7. offer to speak in front of the class?
8. offer to answer questions in class?
9. ask meaningful questions in class?
10. exhibit confidence in his/her school work?
11. persist in his/her school endeavors?
12. talk to others about his/her school work?
13. join in school activities?
14. seek out new things to do in school on his/her own?
15. offer to do extracurricular work in school?
16. spend time helping others?
17. show an interest in others' work?
18. show interest in being a leader?
19. initiate school projects?
20. finish his/her school work?
21. pay attention to class activities?
22. do his/her school work carefully?
23. talk to teachers about personal concerns? (135)*

Other examples can be identified, but these few suggest some of the characteristics teachers may want to look for in observations. Developing a checklist or rating scale from the characteristics has the advantage of providing a guide in observation and is also a systematic method of collecting data. Other observation techniques include anecdotal records, daily diaries, and, possibly, analysis of student autobiographies. All can be useful in making inferences about a student's self-concept if we recognize their limitations.

A second method of diagnosing self-concept is by means of a self-reporting instrument. Such an instrument asks the student to tell about his/her self-concept. As noted previously, the picture received will depend upon what the student wants us to know about his/her self-concept.

---

* William W. Purkey, Bob Cage, and William Graves, "The Florida Key: A Scale to Infer Learner Self-Concept," *Educational and Psychological Measurement* 33 (1973): 979–84. Copyright © 1973. Revised version reprinted by permission of the authors and publisher.

Furthermore, several researchers, most notably Wylie (180), have found that many self-reporting instruments lack desirable levels of validity and reliability. This is especially true for instruments designed to be used with very young children. Nevertheless, these instruments can reveal much about one's self-concept, and, with caution, may be used to make generalized inferences: "In spite of their weaknesses and limitations, self-reports do reveal characteristics of the self and are important to teachers. Used sensitively in conjunction with other evidence, self-reports give rich insights into how the child sees himself and his work" (134).

Sources are available which give complete descriptions, and validity and reliability data for many self-reporting instruments (152, 180). A brief description of some widely used instruments follows.

1. *Thomas Self-Concept Values Test* (Thomas)
   The TSCVT measures fourteen self-value dimensions such as sociability, ability, attractiveness, independence. The 14-item test is designed to be used with young children (4 to 6 years old). However, some caution should be exercised in interpreting test results given the problems of self-concept measurement in young children. (168)
2. *Self-Esteem Inventory* (Coopersmith)
   The 58-item scale was designed by the author to measure general self, social self-peers, home-parents, and school-academic self, in addition to self-esteem. It is worded to be used with children 8 to 10 years old but it has been used successfully with students in grades three through twelve. (42)
3. *Self-Concept of Ability Scale* (Brookover)
   The eight items contained in Form A are designed to measure self-concept of general academic ability; and the eight items in Form B are designed to measure self-perceptions of ability regarding science, mathematics, social studies, and English. The scale is most suitable for use with high-school-age students. (19)
4. *Piers-Harris Children's Self-Concept Scale* (Piers and Harris)
   The 80-item instrument measures general self-concept and may be used for both research and diagnostic work. The simple descriptive statements are designed to measure 10 self-concept dimensions and the scale is appropriate for use in grades three or above. (131)
5. *How I See Myself Scale* (Gordon)
   The HISM consists of 40 (elementary form) or 42 (secondary

form) items developed for use with children ages 3 to 12 years. The scale has been found to measure five self-concept dimensions: physical appearance, interpersonal, teacher-student, academic ability, and autonomy. (78)

6. *Self-Concept Inventory* (Sears)
The revised 48-item scale is designed to measure nine self-concept dimensions and general self-concept. This short, descriptive phrase scale is best suited for use with students age 10 or older. (149)

When using self-reporting instruments, the following points should be remembered:

1. Read the items to very young students.
2. Stress that there are no right or wrong answers.
3. Administer the scale in a nonthreatening manner.
4. Maintain confidentiality of the results. (134)

Planning Strategies for Self-Concept Development

After a careful diagnosis of students' self-concepts, the next task is to plan ways to remediate any low ones and to enhance existing positive ones. How can we best plan for these desired changes? One way is to develop a checklist for periodic reference as we go about our daily activities. Such a checklist might include a series of questions like the following:

Am I projecting an image that tells the student that I am here to build, rather than to destroy, him as a person?

Do I let the student know that I am aware of and interested in him as a unique person?

Do I convey my expectations and confidence that the student can accomplish work, can learn, and is competent?

Do I provide well-defined standards of values, demands for competence, and guidance toward solutions to problems?

When working with parents, do I enhance the academic expectations and evaluations which they hold of their children's ability?

By my behavior, do I serve as a model of authenticity for the student?

Do I take every opportunity to establish a high degree of private or semi-private communication with my students? (134)*

Additional questions suggested by the research reviewed earlier include the following:

Do I encourage students to express their opinions and ideas?

Do I convey to students my concern and interest for their needs?

Do I exhibit a "businesslike and systematic" approach to the learning tasks?

Do I exhibit enthusiasm for the learning tasks and in my classroom interactions?

Do I interject humor into the classroom?

Do I make a concerted effort to interact with all of my students?

Do I encourage my students to praise their peers?

Do I set realistic and challenging expectations for my students?

These and similar questions can be used to guide classroom activities and to provide the basis for a teacher checklist. If we can answer a major part of these questions in the affirmative, then we have set the stage for improving our students' self-concepts.

In addition to these broad guidelines, several specific strategies can be used effectively in the classroom. Many examples have been identified in earlier parts of this book, but before reviewing some of them a few valuable publications deserve mention.

Several books are available which teachers may find very useful as they strive to improve student self-concept. Many offer activities that in one way or another affect self-concept. Others suggest strategies through an analysis and review of selected literature, and some describe specific activities. Among the more widely known are the following:

1. *Self-Concept and School Achievement* (Purkey)
   The book describes the impact of the home environment on the development of self, reviews the literature on the interrelationships between academics and self-concept, and suggests strategies teachers can use to build and reinforce positive self-concepts in students. (134)

---

* William Watson Purkey, *Self-Concept and School Achievement*, © 1970, pp. 49–50. Reprinted by permission of Prentice-Hall, Inc., Englewood Cliffs, N.J.

2. *Enhancing Self-Concept in Early Childhood* (Samuels)
   The author describes the theoretical and empirical literature on self-concept development in very young children and presents practical suggestions for enhancing self-concept. An annotated bibliography lists resources teachers and parents will find useful in working with young children. (144)
3. *Building Positive Self-Concepts* (Felker)
   This book traces the development of self-concept from infancy through adolescence and describes strategies teachers and parents can use to enhance self-concept and self-esteem, and correct negative ones. A specific action program found to be effective by the author is discussed in considerable detail. (62)
4. *Teacher Behavior and Pupil Self-Concept* (Kash and Borich)
   The book describes and analyzes a large number of studies and programs designed to enhance different aspects of a student's general self-concept, placing its primary emphasis on teacher behaviors. The authors also suggest ways to improve the programs and develop more appropriate teacher behaviors. (93)
5. *One Hundred Ways to Enhance Self-Concept in the Classroom: A Handbook for Teachers and Parents* (Canfield and Wells)
   As the title suggests, this book contains 100 activities teachers and parents can use to enhance self-concept. The activities are described in detail, and although most are designed for use with young children, many can be used in the upper grades with only minor modifications necessary. Readers will also find the annotated bibliography of resources beneficial in locating additional materials and activities. (30)

Regarding strategies described earlier, the reader is reminded that researchers have repeatedly found a direct relationship between achievement and self-concept. Moreover, the most recent research in this area has resulted in additonal evidence supporting the claim that improvements in achievement will lead to more positive self-concepts. Considerable attention has been directed to the identification of teaching variables and strategies that will increase academic achievement. Several variables found to be effective are (1) use of praise, (2) use of pupil ideas, (3) frequent questioning, (4) review exercises, (5) clear presentations and questions, (6) teacher enthusiasm, (7) increased time on task, and (8) direct instruction (156).

The variable of direct instruction deserves special attention. It has been defined as follows:

> . . . teachers maintaining a strong academic focus with encouragement and concern for the academic progress of each student; teacher, rather than student, selection of activities; grouping of students into small and large groups for instruction; and using factual questions and controlled practice in teacher-led groups. (137)

Some researchers indicate that direct instructional techniques are effective in increasing achievement (137). Another study concurs but adds that the impact of the techniques varies with grade level and student ability level (22). Thus, teachers who utilize these strategies will produce achivement gains and promote improved self-concept in their students.

Related to these findings regarding direct instruction is the work of two groups of investigators who have developed instructional manuals to be used by teachers for improving student reading and mathematics achievement respectively (24, 75). The manuals give guidelines and suggestions that the teacher may employ in the classroom. Experimental studies have shown that teachers who used the manuals have increased the achievement levels of their students (5, 76).

Mastery learning has also been proposed as a means to improve achievement and self-concept (13). This strategy is based upon the premise that all students can attain a high level of competence if, among other things, their learning difficulties are correctly and systematically identified and appropriate action is taken, sufficient time is allowed for mastery, and the criterion of mastery is clearly stated. Also essential to mastery learning is the development of learning units — manageable units that the student can master and in so doing, increase his/her competence and confidence as a learner. Bloom claims, and there is empirical evidence to support the claim, that by applying mastery learning concepts to the curriculum, students will make not only cognitive gains, but also affective gains (13, 14).

Other strategies for enhancing self-concept are discernible from the research literature. Many have been described in previous sections, but a few merit at least a brief recapping.

One such strategy is the use of praise. As has been mentioned, teacher praise of students is related to achievement and self-concept development. Felker's work reveals that teacher self-praise and peer praise are also instrumental in producing more positive self-images. Felker cautions that these types of praise are difficult to develop and that results will not be visible in the beginning, but continued practice will result in positive gains (62).

A variation of peer verbal praise is the idea of a Happiness Book described earlier (163). Both students and teacher make positive statements about each other. This encourages everyone to focus on the best qualities of an individual and has an advantage over verbal praise in that the individual has a written account that can be referred to periodically.

A third strategy that appears to enhance self-concept is that of self-evaluation. The general self-concept is fairly stable and resistant to change. Through self-evaluation we can help students to see themselves more objectively and to identify behaviors they desire to change. Videotaping and analysis have been found to be particularly good for self-evaluation (71). To a lesser degree audiotaping should work. Considering Felker's work (62), it might prove beneficial for the teacher to model self-evaluation by taping classroom lessons and discussing them with students. By modeling desired behavior, the teacher would be setting the stage for similar student activities.

Teachers may also wish to consider using commercially available affective education programs. Evidence indicates that they can be effective in improving students' interpersonal relationships and self-esteem. No particular program is more effective than others, but as the research shows, the key to success may be extended use. Short-term usage, generally less than six weeks, will probably not produce desired results. Longer periods of exposure will allow time for growth and signal students that the teacher believes it to be an important component of the curriculum and an important part of their development.

Finally, a strategy that deserves much more attention is the cultivation of better parent-teacher partnerships. Parents continue to play a critical role in their children's self-concept development long after they become our students. To put it in negative terms for a moment, parents can undo very quickly all our best plans for enhancing self. On the other hand, by working together in a partnership, parents and teachers can help students develop realistic self-images. By raising their own expectations and creating a home-school environment which encourages students to reach those expectations, parents and teachers can effectively bring about changes. This requires teachers to open up their classrooms to parents, and in many cases it will require teachers to take the initiative in building the bonds with parents. Clearly it is worth the effort to attempt to bring together the two most "significant other" groups children have for the expressed purpose of enhancing their self-concepts.

CONCLUSION

In summary, this publication began by pointing out the importance assigned to the development of positive self-concepts in children. It described the early development of self and general self-concept and then focused attention on the impact of schools in general and teachers in particular on the self-images of youth. A review of the research evidence disclosed that the impact can be a negative one; but we also found that when we make a concerted effort to bring about positive changes, we succeed in many cases. Additional research is needed in many areas, however. There is a great need for a more comprehensive understanding of the construct 'self-concept'. We need to know how it develops, what influences it, how it changes, and how we can measure the changes. Furthermore, we need a great deal more action research to help us identify effective change strategies.

This book has attempted to present a brief statement of the art, and as we await the additional research, it is hoped that its pages have given the reader some insights and suggestions for meeting the challenge of educating the whole child.

References

1. Adams, E. B., and Sarason, I. G. "Relation Between Anxiety in Children and Their Parents." *Child Development* 134 (1963): 237–46.
2. Allen, V. L., et al. "Research on Children Tutoring Children: A Critical Review." *Review of Educational Research* 46 (1976): 355–85.
3. Ammerman, M. S., and Fryrear, J. L. "Photographic Enhancement of Children's Self-Esteem." *Psychology in the Schools* 2 (1975): 319–25.
4. Anderson, H. H., and Brewer, J. E. *Studies of Teachers' Classroom Personalities: II. Effects of Teachers' Dominative Integrative Contacts on Children's Classroom Behavior.* Stanford, Calif.: Stanford University Press, 1946.
5. Anderson, L. M., et al. "An Experimental Study of Effective Teaching in First-Grade Reading Groups." *Elementary School Journal* 79 (1979): 193–223.
6. Ballif, B. L. "The Significance of the Self-Concept in the Knowledge Society." Paper presented at Self-Concept Symposium, Boston, 1978.
7. Bills, R. E. "Sex, Race, and Developmental Differences in Self-Concept Variables as Shown by the Index of Adjustment and Values." Paper presented at Self-Concept Symposium, Boston, 1978.
8. Battle, J. "Self-Esteem of Students in Regular and Special Classes." *Psychological Report* 44 (1979): 212–14.
9. Beals, J. P. "An Investigation of Emotive Perception Among Students in Open Space and Conventional Learning Environments." (Doctoral dissertation, University of Tennessee, 1972.) *Dissertation Abstracts International*, 1973, 33: 5995-A.
10. Becker, W. C., and Englemann, S. *The Oregon District Instructional Model: Comparative Results in Project Follow Through — A Summary of Nine Years of Work.* Eugene: University of Oregon, 1977.
11. Beemer, L. C. "Developmental Changes in the Self-Concepts of Children and Adolescents." (Doctoral dissertation, University of Maryland, 1972.) *Dissertation Abstracts International*, 1972, 32: 5031-A.
12. Bessell, H., and Palomares, U. *Methods in Human Development: Theory Manual and Curriculum Activity Guide.* San Diego: Human Development Training Institute, 1970.
13. Bloom, B. S. *Human Characteristics and School Learning.* New York: McGraw-Hill Book Co., 1976.

14. ———. "Affective Outcomes of School Leaning." *Phi Delta Kappan* 59 (1977): 193–98.

15. Borg, W. R. *Ability Grouping in the Public Schools.* Madison, Wis.: Dembar Educational Research Services, 1966.

16. Brady, P. J., et al. "Predicting Student Self-Concept, Anxiety, and Responsibility from Self-Evaluation and Self-Praise." *Psychology in the Schools* 15 (1978): 434–38.

17. Briggs, L. D. "The Impact of Failure on Elementary School Pupils." (Doctoral dissertation, North Texas State University, 1966.) *Dissertation Abstracts International,* 1967, 27: 2719-A.

18. Broedel, J., et al. "The Effects of Group Counseling on Gifted Underachieving Adolescents." *Journal of Counseling Psychology* 7 (1960): 163–70.

19. Brookover, W. B., et al. *Self-Concept of Ability and School Achievement II: Improving Academic Achievement Through Students' Self-Concept Enhancement.* U. S. Office of Education, Cooperative Research Project No. 1636. East Lansing: Office of Research and Publications, Michigan State University, 1965.

20. ———, and Erickson, E. L. *Society, Schools, and Learning.* Boston: Allyn and Bacon, 1969.

21. ———, and Passalacqua, J. "Comparisons of Aggregate Self-Concepts for Populations with Different Reference Groups." Paper presented at Self-Concept Symposium, Boston, 1978.

22. Brophy, J. E. *Advances in Teacher Effectiveness Research.* Occasional Paper No. 18. East Lansing: Institute for Research on Teaching, Michigan State University, 1979.

23. ———, and Good, T. L. "Teachers' Communication of Differential Expectations for Children's Classroom Performance: Some Behavioral Data." *Journal of Educational Psychology* 61 (1970): 365–74.

24. ———, et al. *An Instructional Model for First Grade Reading Groups.* Report No. 4043. Research and Development Center for Teacher Education, University of Texas at Austin, 1976.

25. Brown, P. "A Comparison of Self-Esteem, Anxiety, and Behavior of Black and Non-Black Under-Achieving Elementary School Students in Open and Stratified Classrooms." (Doctoral dissertation, Columbia University, 1973.) *Dissertation Abstracts International,* 1973, 34: 3011-A.

26. Burchinal, L., et al. "Children's Personality Adjustment and Social-Economic Status in their Families." *Journal of Genetic Psychology* 92 (1958): 149–59.

27. Calhoun, G., Jr., and Morse, W. C. "Self-Concept and Self-Esteem: Another Persepective." *Psychology in the Schools* 14 (1973): 318–22.

28. Callison, C. P. "Experimental Induction of Self-Concept." *Psychological Reports* 35 (1974): 1235–38.

29. Calsyn, R. J., and Kenny, D. A. "Self-Concept of Ability and Perceived Evaluation of Others: Cause or Effect of Academic Achievement?" *Journal of Educational Psychology* 69 (1977): 136–45.

30. Canfield, J., and Wells, H. C. *One Hundred Ways to Enhance Self-Concept in the Classroom: A Handbook for Teachers and Parents.* Englewood Cliffs, N.J.: Prentice-Hall, 1976.

31. Carlson, R. K. "Raising Self-Concepts of Disadvantaged Children Through Puppetry." *Elementary English* 47 (1970): 349–55.

32. Chansky, N. M. "Progress of Promoted and Repeating Grade I Failures." *Journal of Experimental Education* 32 (1964): 225–37.

33. Clark, B. B., and Trowbridge, N. T. "Encouraging Creativity Through Inservice Teacher Education." *Journal of Research and Development in Education* 4 (1971): 87–94.

34. Coleman, J. S., et al. *Equality of Educational Opportunity.* Washington, D. C.: Government Printing Office, 1966.

35. Combs, A. W., et al. "The Measurement of Self-Concept and Self-Report." *Educational and Psychological Measurement* 23 (1963): 493–500.

36. ———. "Some Observations on Self-Concept Research and Theory." Paper presented at Self-Concept Symposium, Boston, 1978.

37. Combs, C. F. "A Study of the Relationship Between Certain Perceptions of Self and Scholastic Underachievement in Academically Capable High School Boys." (Doctoral dissertation, Syracuse University, 1963.) *Dissertation Abstracts International*, 1963, 24: 620-A.

38. Combs, H. A., and Snygg, D. *Individual Behavior.* New York: Harper, 1959.

39. Commission on the Reorganization of Secondary Education. *Cardinal Principles of Secondary Education.* Bulletin No. 35. Washington, D.C.: Government Printing Office, 1918.

40. Cookston, H. M., and Mason, B. O. "Recent Studies on Self-Concept in Elementary Students." *Educational Leadership* 34 (1977): 639–41.

41. Cooley, C. H. *Human Nature and the Social Order.* New York: Charles Scribner and Sons, 1902.

42. Coopersmith, S. *The Antecedents of Self-Esteem.* San Francisco: W. H. Freeman and Co., 1967.

43. Darrigrand, G., and Gum, M. "A Comparison of the Effects of Two Methods of Developmental Guidance on the Self-Concept, Peer Relationships, and School Attitudes of Second-Grade Children." In *Additional Studies in Elementary School Guidance: Psychological Education Activities Evaluated*, edited by G. Miller, pp. 71–84. St. Paul: Minnesota Department of Education, 1973.

44. Davidson, H. H., and Lang, G. "Children's Perceptions of Their Teachers' Feelings Toward Them Related to Self-Perception, School Achievement, and Behavior." *Journal of Experimental Education* 29 (1960): 107–18.

45. Day, R. W. "An Investigation of the Effects of the *Human Development Program* 'Magic Circle' on Selected Affective, Cognitive, and Confluent Variables of Second, Fourth, and Sixth Graders." (Doctoral dissertation, University of Alabama, 1977.) *Dissertation Abstracts International*, 1978, 39: 125–26-A.

46. DeBlaissie, R. R., and Healy, G. W. *Self-Concept: A Comparison of Spanish-American, Negro, and Anglo Adolescents Across Ethnic, Sex, and Socioeconomic Variables*. Las Cruces, N.M.: ERIC Clearinghouse on Rural Education and Small Schools, 1970.

47. Deutsch, M. *Minority Group and Class Status as Related to Social and Personality Factors in Scholastic Achievement*. Ithaca, N.Y.: Cornell University Press, 1960.

48. Dinkmeyer, D. *Developing Understanding of Self and Others*. Circle Pines, Minn.: American Guidance Service, 1970.

49. Drews, E. M. "The Effectiveness of Homogenous and Heterogenous Ability Grouping in Ninth Grade English Classes with Slow, Average and Superior Students." Unpublished manuscript, Michigan State University, 1962.

50. Dreyer, A. S., and Haupt, D. "Self-Evaluation in Young Children." *Journal of Genetic Psychology* 108 (1966): 185–97.

51. Drowne, J. L. "Three Group Counseling Approaches." *Elementary School Guidance and Counseling* 6 (1972): 291–93.

52. Dunn, J. A. "The Effect of Creative Dramatics on the Oral Language Abilities and Self-Esteem of Blacks, Chicanos, and Anglos in the Second and Fifth Grades." (Doctoral dissertation, University of Colorado at Boulder, 1977.) *Dissertation Abstracts International*, 1978, 38: 3907-A.

53. Durr, W. K., and Schmatz, R. R. "Personality Differences Between High-Achieving and Low-Achieving Gifted Children." *Reading Teacher* 17 (1964): 251–54.

54. Edeburn, C. E. "An Analysis of Self-Concept in Two Elementary Schools in Relationship to Sex, Grade Level, and Teacher." (Doctoral dissertation, University of North Dakota, 1973.) *Dissertation Abstracts International*, 1974, 34: 4554-A.

55. ———, and Landry, R. G. "Teacher Self-Concept and Student Self-Concept." Paper presented at the Annual Conference of American Educational Research Association, Chicago, 1974.

56. Edmondson, R. J. "A Comparison of Two Different Instructional Approaches in Achieving Self-Concepts of Fourth Grade Students in a Public School." (Doctoral dissertation, Nova University, 1976.) *Dissertation Abstracts International*, 1978, 38: 4580-A.

57. Educational Policies Commission. *The Purposes of Education in American Democracy*. Washington, D.C.: National Education Association, 1938.

58. Elaugh, C., and Harlow, H. "Behavior of Male and Female Teachers as Related to Behaviors and Attitudes of Elementary School Children." Peoria, Ill.: Bradley University, 1973. (ERIC Document ED 086 345)

59. Elder, G. H. "Adolescent Socialization and Development." In *Handbook of Personality Theory and Research*, edited by E. F. Borgatta and W. W. Lambert, pp. 239–364. Chicago: Rand, McNally, 1968.

60. Farls, R. J. "High and Low Achievement of Intellectually Average Intermediate Grade Students Related to the Self-Concept and Social Approval." *Dissertation Abstracts International*, 1967, 28: 1205-A.

61. Farquhar, W. W. *A Comprehensive Study of the Motivational Factors Underlying Achievement of Eleventh-Grade High School Students.* U. S. Office of Education, Cooperative Research Project No. 846. East Lansing: Office of Research and Publications, Michigan State University, 1968.

62. Felker, D. W. *Building Positive Self-Concepts.* Minneapolis, Minn.: Burgess Publishing Co., 1974.

63. ———, et al. "The Effects of a Teacher Program in Self-Concept Enhancement on Pupils' Self-Concept, Anxiety, and Intellectual Achievement Responsibility." *Journal of Educational Research* 66 (1973): 443–45.

64. Fink, M. B. "Self-Concept as It Relates to Academic Achievement." *California Journal of Educational Research* 13 (1962): 57–62.

65. Finlayson, H. J. "Nonpromotion and Self-Concept Development." *Phi Delta Kappan* 59 (1977): 205–6.

66. Finley, M. "Development of Social Awareness in First-Grade Children." Unpublished manuscript, Middle Tennessee State University, 1972.

67. Fitts, W. H. *The Tennessee Self-Concept Scale.* Nashville: Counselor Recordings and Tests, 1964.

68. ———. "Issues Regarding Self-Concept Change." Paper presented at Self-Concept Symposium, Boston, 1978.

69. Fromm, E. "Selfishness and Self-Love." *Psychiatry* 2 (1939): 507–23.

70. Gardner, W. E. "Compeer Assistance Through Tutoring and Group Guidance Activities." *Urban Review* 10 (1978): 45–54.

71. Garner, G. "Modifying Pupil Self-Concept and Behavior." *Today's Education* 63 (1974): 26–28.

72. Gergan, K. J. *The Concept of Self.* New York: Holt, Rinehart, and Winston, 1971.

73. Germain, R. B. "Self-Concept and Self-Esteem Reexamined." *Psychology in the Schools* 15 (1978): 386–90.

74. Gibby, R. G., and Gibby, S. R. "The Effects of Stress Resulting from Academic Failure." *Journal of Clinical Psychology* 23 (1967): 35–37.

75. Good, T. L., et al. *Teachers Manual: Missouri Mathematics Effectiveness Project.* Columbia: Center for Research in Social Behavior, University of Missouri, 1977.

76. ———, and Grouws, D. A. "The Missouri Mathematics Effectiveness Project: An Experimental Study in Fourth-Grade Classrooms." *Journal of Educational Psychology* 71 (1979): 355–62.

77. Goodlad, J. I. *What Schools Are For.* Bloomington, Ind.: Phi Delta Kappa Educational Foundation, 1979.

78. Gordon, I. J. *A Test Manual for the How I See Myself Scale.* Gainesville: Florida Educational Research and Development Council, 1968.

79. Griffin, J. L. "The Effects of Integration on Academic Aptitude, Classroom Achievement, Self-Concept, and Attitudes Toward the School Environment of a

Selected Group of Negro Students in Tulsa, Oklahoma." (Doctoral dissertation, University of Tulsa, 1969.) *Dissertation Abstracts International*, 1969, 30: 1748-A.

80. Grove, E. H. "An Investigation of the Effects of Multi-Age Grouping on Student Attitude." (Doctoral dissertation, Washington State University, 1978.) *Dissertation Abstracts International*, 1978, 39: 663-A.

81. Hansen, J. C., et al. "A Study of the Relationships in Multiple Counseling." *Journal of Educational Research* 60 (1967): 461–63.

82. Harootunian, B. "Self-Other Relationships of Segregated and Desegregated Ninth Graders." Paper presented at Annual Conference of American Educational Research Association, Chicago, 1968.

83. Hawkinson, A. "The Effect of the HDP on the Self-Concept of Some Elementary School Children." Master's thesis, California State University, 1970.

84. Helper, M. M. "Parental Evaluation of Children and Children's Self-Evaluations." *Journal of Abnormal and Social Psychology* 56 (1958): 190–94.

85. Henderson, G. "An Analysis of Self-Concept of Academic Ability as Related to Social Psychological Variables Comprising School Climate in Black and White Elementary Children with Differential School Settings." (Doctoral dissertation, Michigan State University, 1973.) *Dissertation Abstracts International*, 1974, 34: 3560-A.

86. Hodgkins, B. J., and Stakenas, R. G. "A Study of Self-Concepts of Negro and White Youths in Segregated Environments." *Journal of Negro Education* 38 (1969): 370–77.

87. Hopke, M. E. "A Comparison of Basic Skills Achievement Level, Attitude Toward School, Academic and Global Self-Concepts of Open Concept Primary Grade School Students and Traditional Self-Contained Classroom Primary Grade School Students." (Doctoral dissertation, University of Washington, 1974.) *Dissertation Abstracts International*, 1975, 35: 7181–82-A.

88. Horne, M. D. "Attitudes and Mainstreaming: A Literature Review for School Psychologists." *Psychology in the Schools* 16 (1979): 61–67.

89. Horwitz, R. A. "Psychological Effects of the 'Open Classroom'." *Review of Educational Research* 49 (1979): 71–86.

90. Hunt, T. C., and Yarusso, L. C. "Open Education: Can It Survive Its Critics?" *Peabody Journal of Education* 56 (1979): 294–300.

91. Johnson, A. A. "A Study of the Relationship Between Nonpromotion and the Male Student's Self-Concept of Academic Ability and His Perceived Parental, Friends' and Teachers' Evaluation of His Academic Ability." (Doctoral dissertation, Michigan State University, 1968.) *Dissertation Abstracts International*, 1968, 29: 409-A.

92. Junell, J. S. "An Analysis of the Effects of Multigrading on a Number of Noncognitive Variables." (Doctoral dissertation, University of Washington, 1970.) *Dissertation Abstracts International*, 1971, 32: 94-A.

93. Kash, M. M., and Borich, G. D. *Teacher Behavior and Pupil Self-Concept*. Reading, Mass.: Addison-Wesley Publishing Co., 1978.

94. Katz, I. "The Socialization of Academic Motivation in Minority Group Children." In *Nebraska Symposium on Motivation*, edited by D. Levine, pp. 133–91. Lincoln: University of Nebraska Press, 1967.

95. Keller, S. "The Social World of the Urban Slum Child: Some Preliminary Findings." *American Journal of Orthopsychiatry* 33 (1963): 823–31.

96. Kifer, E. "The Effects of School Achievement on the Affective Traits of the Learner." Paper presented at Annual Conference of American Educational Research Association, New Orleans, 1973.

97. Kinsella, R. J. "A Study of the Effects of Increased Social Acceptability on Fourth Grade Students' Self-Concept." (Doctoral dissertation, Syracuse University, 1977.) *Dissertation Abstracts International*, 1978, 39: 578-A.

98. Klein, M. F., et al. "A Study of Schooling: Curriculum." *Phi Delta Kappan* 61 (1979): 244–48.

99. Koskoff, C. G. "A Comparison of the Self-Concept of Children Enrolled in American Open Primary Schools and American Traditional Schools." (Doctoral dissertation, University of Connecticut, 1973.) *Dissertation Abstracts International*. 1974, 34: 1486-A.

100. Lewin, K., et al. "Patterns of Aggressive Behavior in Experimentally Created 'Social Climates'." *Journal of Social Psychology* 10 (1939): 271–99.

101. Lewis, G. M. "Interpersonal Relations and School Achievement." *Children* 2 (1964): 235–36.

102. Limbacher, W. *Dimensions of Personality*. Dayton, Ohio: Pflaum, 1973.

103. Linton, T. H. "A Study of the Relationship of Global Self-Concept, Academic Self-Concept, and Academic Achievement Among Anglo and Mexican-American Sixth Grade Students." Paper presented at the Annual Conference of American Educational Research Association, Chicago, 1972.

104. Livingston-White, D. J. "The Relation of Tracking and Self-Esteem Among Eighth-Grade Students." *Phi Delta Kappan* 58 (1976): 282–83.

105. Long, B. H., and Henderson, E. H. "Self-Social Concepts of Disadvantaged School Beginners." *Journal of Genetic Psychology* 113 (1968): 41–51.

106. Lovin, J. C. "The Effects of the School's Physical Environment on the Self-Concepts of Elementary School Students." (Doctoral dissertation, University of Georgia, 1972.) *Dissertation Abstracts International*, 1973, 33: 4744-A.

107. McCarthy, J. D., and Yancey, W. L. "Uncle Tom and Mr. Charlie: Metaphysical Pathos in the Study of Racism and Personal Disorganization." *American Journal of Sociology* 76 (1971): 648–72.

108. McHenry, D. F. "A Comparison of the Self-Concept of Leaving Disabled Children in Three Special Program Structures." (Doctoral dissertation, Kansas State University, 1977.) *Dissertation Abstracts International*, 1977, 38: 3416-A.

109. Mahler, M. S. "Thoughts About Development and Individuation." *Psychoanalytic Study of the Child* 18 (1963): 307–24.

110. Manis, M. "Personal Adjustment, Assumed Similarity to Parents, and Inferred Parental Evaluations of the Self." *Journal of Consulting Psychology* 22 (1958): 481–85.

111. Mann, M. "What Does Ability Grouping Do to the Self-Concept?" *Childhood Education* 26 (1960): 357–60.

112. Marshall, P. "Effective Counselor Uses of DUSO Guidance Materials." *Guidelines for Pupil Services* 12 (1973): 20–23.

113. Mason, B. O. "The Effect of University Tutors on the Self-Concepts of Elementary School Pupils." (Doctoral dissertation, Louisiana State University, 1975.) *Dissertation Abstracts International*, 1976, 36: 4245-A.

114. Mead, G. H. *Mind, Self, and Society*. Chicago: University of Chicago Press, 1934.

115. Medinnus, G. R., and Curtis, E. J. "The Relation Between Maternal Self-Acceptance and Child Acceptance." *Journal of Consulting Psychology* 27 (1963): 542–44.

116. Medway, F. J., and Smith, R. C., Jr. "An Examination of Contemporary Elementary School Affective Education Programs." *Psychology in the Schools* 15 (1978): 260–69.

117. Minuchin, P., et al. *The Psychological Impact of School Experience: A Comparative Study of Nine-Year-Old Children in Contrasting Schools*. New York: Basic Books, 1969.

118. Mitchell, D. E., and Spady, W. G. "Organizational Contexts for Implementing Outcome Based Education." *Educational Researcher* 7 (1978): 9–17.

119. Mohan, M. *Peer Tutoring as a Technique for Teaching the Unmotivated, A Research Report*. Fredonia, N.Y.: Teacher Education Research Center, University College, 1972.

120. Morgan, R. F., and Toy, T. B. "Learning by Teaching: A Student-to-Student Compensatory Tutoring Program in a Rural School System and Its Relevance to the Educational Cooperative." *Psychological Record* 206 (1970): 159–69.

121. Morse, W. G. "Self-Concept in the School Setting." *Childhood Education* 41 (1964): 195–98.

122. Mosser, M., and Evans, R. "The Effects of Small Group Interaction on Self-Esteem and Interpersonal Relations." Unpublished manuscript, Palm Beach County Public Schools, Florida, 1973.

123. National Commission on Resources for Youth, Inc. *An Evaluation of the Youth Tutoring Youth Model for In-School Neighborhood Youth Corps*. New York, 1972.

124. Northern California Program Development Center. "Goal Card." Chico, California, 1971.

125. Ontario-Montclair School District. *Final Report on Cross-Age Teaching*. Report No. 68-061380. Ontario, Calif. 1968–71.

126. Parker, J. L. "Enhancing Self-Concept Through TV Media." *Elementary School Guidance and Counseling* 9 (1975): 246–48.

127. Pate, T. L. "An Investigation of the Effects of Creative Drama upon Reading Ability, Verbal Growth, Vocabulary Development, and Self-Concept of Secondary School Students." (Doctoral dissertation, East Texas State University, 1977.) *Dissertation Abstracts International*, 1978, 38: 6506-A.

128. Payne, B. F., and Dunn, C. J. "Using Group Counseling to Alter Self-Concepts of Culturally Different Elementary Children." *Childhood Education* 47 (1970): 107–8.

129. Peck, R. F., et al. "Teacher Effects on Student Achievement and Self-Esteem." Paper presented at Annual Conference of American Educational Research Association, New York, 1977.

130. Pepitone, A. *Attraction and Hostility*. New York: Prentice-Hall, 1964.

131. Piers, E. V., and Harris, D. B. *Piers-Harris Children's Self-Concept Scale*. Nashville, Tenn.: Counselor Recordings and Tests, 1969.

132. Poris, M. A. "The Relationships Among Specific Teacher Behaviors, Student Self-Concept, and Student Divergent Production." (Doctoral dissertation, Hofstra University, 1977.) *Dissertation Abstracts International*, 1977, 38: 3274-A.

133. Poudrier, B. R. "The Effect of a Self-Concept Intervention Program on the Self-Esteem and Achievement of Fourth Graders." (Doctoral dissertation, University of Virginia, 1975.) *Dissertation Abstracts International*, 1976, 36: 4405-A.

134. Purkey, W. W. *Self-Concept and School Achievement*. Englewood Cliffs, N.J.: Prentice-Hall, 1970.

135. ———, et al. "The Florida Key: A Scale to Infer Learner Self-Concept." *Educational and Psychological Measurement* 33 (1973): 979–84.

136. Rogers, C. *Casebook of Non-Directive Counseling*. Boston: Houghton Mifflin, 1947.

137. Rosenshine, B. V. "Content, Time, and Direct Instruction." In *Research on Teaching: Concepts, Findings, and Implications*, edited by P. L. Peterson and H. J. Walberg, pp. 28–56. Berkeley, Calif.: McCutchan Publishing Corp., 1979.

138. Rosenberg, M. *Society and the Adolescent Self Image*. Princeton, N.J.: Princeton University Press, 1965.

139. Rowe, M. B. "Science, Silence, and Sanctions." *Science and Children* 7 (1969): 11–13.

140. Rusch, R., and Dinkmeyer, D. "Developing Understanding of Self and Others and the Appropriate Experimental Guidance Model." Unpublished manuscript, State University of New York at Albany, 1973.

141. Ryans, D. G. *Characteristics of Teachers*. Washington, D.C.: American Council on Education, 1960.

142. Sackett, J. W. "A Comparison of Self-Concept and Achievement of Sixth-Grade Students in an Open Space School, Self-Contained School, and Departmentalized School." (Doctoral dissertation, University of Iowa, 1971.) *Dissertation Abstracts International*, 1971, 32: 2372-A.

143. Samuels, S. C. "An Investigation into the Self-Concepts of Lower and Middle Class Black and White Kindergarten Children." *Journal of Negro Education* 42 (1973): 467–72.

144. ———. *Enhancing Self-Concept in Early Childhood*. New York: Human Sciences Press, 1977.

145. ———, et al. *The Influence of Team Teaching and Flexible Grouping on Attitudes of Junior High*

School Students, Final Report. Albany: New York State Experimental and Innovative Programs, New York State Board of Education, Division of Research, 1969.

146. Sarason, S., et al. *Anxiety in Elementary School Children.* New York: John Wiley and Sons, 1960.

147. Scheirer, M. A., and Kraut, R. E. "Increasing Educational Achievement Via Self-Concept Change." *Review of Educational Research* 49 (1979): 131–50.

148. Sears, R. R. "Relations of Early Socialization Experience to Self-Concepts and Gender Role in Middle Childhood." *Child Development* 41 (1970): 267–89.

149. Sears, P. S. "The Effect of Classroom Conditions on the Strength of Achievement Motive and Work Output on Elementary School Children." USOE Cooperative Research Report: Project No. OE-873. Stanford, Calif.: Stanford University, 1963.

150. Sears, R. R., et al. *Patterns of Child Rearing.* New York: Row and Peterson, 1957.

151. Sewell, W. H., and Haller, A. O. "Social Status and Personality Adjustment of the Child." *Sociometry* 19 (1965): 114–25.

152. Shavelson, R., et al. "Self-Concept: Validation of Construct Interpretations." *Review of Educational Research* 46 (1976): 407–41.

153. Shaw, M. C. "Definition and Identification of Academic Underachievers." In *Guidance for the Underachiever with Superior Ability,* edited by L. M. Miller, pp. 15–27. Washington, D.C.: Government Printing Office, 1961.

154. ———, and Alves, G. J. "The Self-Concept of Bright Academic Underachievers: Continued." *Personnel and Guidance Journal* 42 (1963): 401–3.

155. Silberman, C. E. *Crisis in the Classroom: The Remaking of American Education.* New York: Random House, 1970.

156. Silvernail, D. L. *Teaching Styles as Related to Student Achievement.* Washington, D.C.: National Education Association, 1979.

157. ———. "Educational Goals: Which Ones Are Most and Least Important to Administrators and Teachers?" *NASSP Bulletin* (in press).

158. Silverstein, B., and Krate, R. *Children of the Dark Ghetto: A Development Psychology.* New York: Prager Publishers, 1975.

159. Smirnoff, V. *The Scope of Child Analysis.* New York: International Universities Press, 1971.

160. Spaulding, R. L. "Achievement, Creativity, and Self-Concept Correlates of Teacher-Pupil Transactions in Elementary Schools." In *Readings in Child Behavior,* 2d ed., edited by C. B. Stendler, pp. 313–18. New York: Harcourt, Brace and World, 1964.

161. Stenner, A. J., and Katzenmeyer, W. G. "Self-Concept Development in Young Children." *Phi Delta Kappan* 58 (1976): 356–57.

162. Stern, T. M. "A Study of the Use of Freshman and Sophomore Elementary Education Majors as Reading Tutors to Disadvantaged Elementary School Students." (Doctoral dissertation, University of Georgia, 1978.) *Dissertation Abstracts International,* 1978, 39: 7148-A.

163. Stilwell, W. E., and Barclay, J. R. "Effects of Affective Education Interventions in the Elementary School." *Psychology in the Schools* 16 (1979): 80–87.

164. Strickler, R. "Evaluation of HDP and Other Guidance Materials." Unpublished manuscript, Penn-Delco School District, Acton, Penn., 1973.

165. Sullivan, H. S. *The Interpersonal Theory of Psychiatry*. New York: Norton, 1953.

166. Survant, A. "Building Positive Self-Concepts." *Instructor* 81 (1972): 94–95.

167. Thomas, J. B. *Self-Concept in Psychology and Education: A Review of Research*. Windsor, Berks: NFER Publishing Co., 1973.

168. Thomas, W. L. *The Thomas Self-Concept Values Test*. Detroit, Mich.: Educational Services Co., 1969.

169. Tocco, T. S., and Bridges, C. M., Jr. "Mother-Child Self-Concept Transmission in Florida Model Follow-Through Participants." Paper presented at Annual Conference of American Educational Research Association, New York, 1971.

170. Trowbridge, N. T. "Self-Concept and Socio-Economic Class." *Psychology in the Schools* 7 (1970): 3.

171. ———. "Self-Concept and Socio-Economic Status in Elementary School Children." *American Educational Research Journal* 9 (1972): 525–37.

172. Valero-Figueira, E. "An Exploration of the Achievement, Self-Concept, and School Morale of Emotionally Disturbed Children in Different Special Educational Settings." (Doctoral dissertation, University of Michigan, 1978.) *Dissertation Abstracts International*, 1978, 39: 3521-A.

173. Venson, G. M. "The Effects of Time-Related Modern Educational Dance Programs on the Self-Concept of Fourth, Fifth, and Sixth Grade Girls in a Southern Urban City." (Doctoral dissertation, Southern Illinois University at Carbondale, 1977.) *Dissertation Abstracts International*, 1977, 38: 2569-A.

174. Washington, K. R. "Self-Concept Development: An Affective Educational Experience for Inner-City Teachers." *Young Children* 19 (1974): 305–10.

175. White, K., and Howard, J. L. "Failure to Be Promoted and Self-Concept Among Elementary School Children." *Elementary School Guidance and Counseling* 7 (1973): 182–87.

176. Williams, R. L., and Cole, S. "Self-Concept and School Adjustment." *Personnel and Guidance Journal* 46 (1968): 478–81.

177. Withall, J. "The Development of a Technique for the Measurement of Social-Emotional Climate in Classrooms." *Journal of Experimental Education* 17 (1949): 347–61.

178. Withycombe, J. S. "An Analysis of the Differences by Sex, Grade Level, and Painte Indian Matriculation on Self-Concept, Social Status (Other Perceived), and Social Status (Self-Perceived) of Painte Indian and White Elementary School Children in Nevada." (Doctoral dissertation, University of Connecticut, 1970.) *Dissertation Abstracts International*, 1971, 31: 6420-A.

179. Wylie, R. C. "Children's Estimates of Their Schoolwork Ability as a Function of Sex, Race, and Socioeconomic Level." *Journal of Personality* 31 (1963): 203–24.

180. ———. *The Self-Concept: A Review of Methodological Considerations and Measuring Instruments.* Rev. ed. Lincoln: University of Nebraska Press, 1974.

181. Yamamoto, J. Y., and Klentschy, M. "An Examination of Intergrade Tutoring Experience on Attitudinal Development of Inner-City Children." Paper presented at meeting of California Educational Research Association, San Jose, 1972.

182. Yeatts, P. P. "An Analysis of Developmental Changes in the Self-Report of Negro and White Children, Grades Three Through Twelve." (Doctoral dissertation, University of Florida, 1967.) *Dissertation Abstracts International,* 1968, 29: 823-A.

183. Young, R. "A Study of the Effectiveness of DUSO Kit Experiences on Some Primary Children." Unpublished manuscript, Mental Health, British Columbia, Vancouver, B.C., 1973.

184. Zirkel, P. A. "Self-Concept and the 'Disadvantaged' of Ethnic Group Membership and Mixture." *Review of Educational Research* 41 (1971): 211–25.

185. ———, and Greene, J. F. "The Measurement of the Self-Concept of Disadvantaged Students." Paper presented at Annual Conference of National Council on Measurement in Education, New York, 1971.

186. ———, and Moses, E. G. "Self-Concept and Ethnic Group Membership Among Public School Students." *American Educational Research Journal* 8 (1971): 253–65.